Ika Syntax

Studies in the Languages of Colombia 1

Summer Institute of Linguistics and
The University of Texas at Arlington
Publications in Linguistics

Publication 93

Editors

Virgil Poulter
University of Texas
at Arlington

William R. Merrifield
Summer Institute of
Linguistics

Assistant Editors

Alan C. Wares

Iris M. Wares

Consulting Editors

Doris A. Bartholomew
Pamela M. Bendor-Samuel
Desmond C. Derbyshire
Robert A. Dooley
Jerold A. Edmondson

Austin Hale
Robert E. Longacre
Eugene E. Loos
Kenneth L. Pike
Viola G. Waterhouse

Ika Syntax
Studies in the Languages of Colombia 1

Paul Frank

A Publication of
The Summer Institute of Linguistics
and
The University of Texas at Arlington
1990

© 1990 by the Summer Institute of Linguistics, Inc.
Library of Congress Catalog No: 90–071095
ISBN: 0–88312–801–2
ISSN: 1040–0850

All Rights Reserved

No part of this publication may be reproduced, stored in a retrieval system, or transmitted in any form or by any means—electronic, mechanical, photocopy, recording, or otherwise—without the express permission of the Summer Institute of Linguistics, with the exception of brief excerpts in journal articles or reviews.

Cover design and sketch by Jonathan Gregerson

Copies of this and other publications of the Summer Institute of Linguistics may be obtained from

        International Academic Bookstore
        Summer Institute of Linguistics
        7500 W. Camp Wisdom Rd.
        Dallas, TX 75236

Contents

Map x

Foreword xi

Abbreviations xiii

1 Introduction
- 1.1 The genetic classification of the Ika language 1
- 1.2 The Bíntukwa people 1
- 1.3 The source of data for this study 2
- 1.4–14 The typological characteristics of Ika
- 1.4 Word order 3
- 1.5 Adpositions 3
- 1.6 Head noun and adjective 3
- 1.7 Head noun and genitive 4
- 1.8 Affixation 4
- 1.9 Relative clauses 5
- 1.10 Comparatives 6

1.11 Negation 6
1.12 Questions 6
1.13 Coding of major syntactic functions 7
1.14 Ergativity 8
1.15 Ika phonology 10
    1.16–19 Ika morphophonemics
1.16 Phonologically conditioned variation 12
1.17 Alternations applying only at morpheme boundaries 14
1.18 Vowel/∅ alternations 15
1.19 Morphophonemic fusion 18

2 Word Classes in Ika
2.1 Nouns 19
2.2 Adjectives 19
    2.3–10 Verbs
2.3 Intransitive verbs 20
2.4 Transitive verbs 20
2.5 Bitransitive verbs 21
2.6 Impersonal verbs 22
2.7 Verbs with sentential objects 22
2.8 Quotation-like verbs .23
2.9 Copular verbs 23
2.10 Auxiliary verbs 24
2.11 Adverbs 25
2.12 Pronouns 25
2.13 Noun adjuncts 26
2.14 Verb adjuncts 27
2.15 Conjunctions 27
2.16 Postpositions 27

3 The Noun Phrase

- 3.1 Quantifiers 29
- 3.2 Numerals 30
- 3.3 Adjectives 32
- 3.4 Articles 33
- 3.5 Case marking 33
- 3.6 Nouns as modifiers .33

4 Case Marking and Postpositional Phrases

- 4.1 *-se?* 'locative, source/goal, ergative' 36
- 4.2 *-sin* 'instrument, accompaniment, and conjunction' 37
- 4.3 *-ikin* 'limitative' 38
- 4.4 *-eki* 'locative' 39
- 4.5 *-aba?* 'location' and 'time' 40
- 4.6 *-n* 'by means of' 41
- 4.7 *zei* 'genitive' 41
- 4.8 *pari* 'from' 43
- 4.9 *zani* 'to be from' 43
- 4.10 Other markers of position 44

5 The Verb Phrase

- 5.1 Auxiliary verbs 46
- 5.2 Agreement 50
- 5.3 Locationals and noun classes 53
- 5.4 Temporal aspect 56
- 5.5–10 Modal suffixes
- 5.5 *-ikua* (obligation) 59
- 5.6 *-ikuei* (ability) 59
- 5.7 *-wi?na* (prohibition) .60

5.8 *-iwa* (intention) 60
5.9 *-ngua* (future) and *-nguasi* (purpose) 61
5.10 *-iza* (result) 62
5.11 Deictic suffixes 63
    5.12–15 Valence change
5.12 Causatives 66
5.13 *kʌ-* (peripheral participant) and valence increase 68
5.14 Benefactives 70
5.15 Reciprocals and reflexives 71
5.16 Comparatives and equatives 72
5.17 *an-* (reference) 73

6 Clause Formation

6.1 Declaratives 77
    6.2–3 Questions
6.2 Yes/No questions 79
6.3 Content questions 82
    6.4–6 Imperatives
6.4 Immediate imperatives .87
6.5 Future imperatives 88
6.6 Hortatory 88
6.7 Negation 89

7 Sentence Formation

7.1 Temporal clause connectors 92
7.2 Logical clause connectors 94
7.3 Sentence introducers 95

8 Subordination

8.1 Relative clauses 99

- 8.2 Locative nominalized clauses ... 102
- 8.3–8 Complementation
- 8.3 Verbs with full sentence complements ... 103
- 8.4 Verbs with complements not marked for mood ... 105
- 8.5 Indirect questions ... 106
- 8.6 Motion verbs with purpose complements ... 107
- 8.7 Resultant state complements ... 108
- 8.8 *aʔdžun* 'want' ... 109
- 8.9 Adverbial clauses of simultaneous action ... 110

9 Pragmatics

- 9.1 Nonreferential subjects ... 113
- 9.2 Off-stage subjects ... 114
- 9.3 Ergative marking of agent noun phrases ... 115
- 9.4 Focus ... 119
- 9.5–9.9 The pragmatics of clause organization
- 9.5 Zero anaphora ... 121
- 9.6 The linear order of clause constituents ... 123
- 9.7 *-ri* (topic) ... 124
- 9.8 Participant reference ... 128
- 9.9 Optional auxiliary verbs and pragmatic structuring ... 132

10 Conclusion ... 135

References ... 137

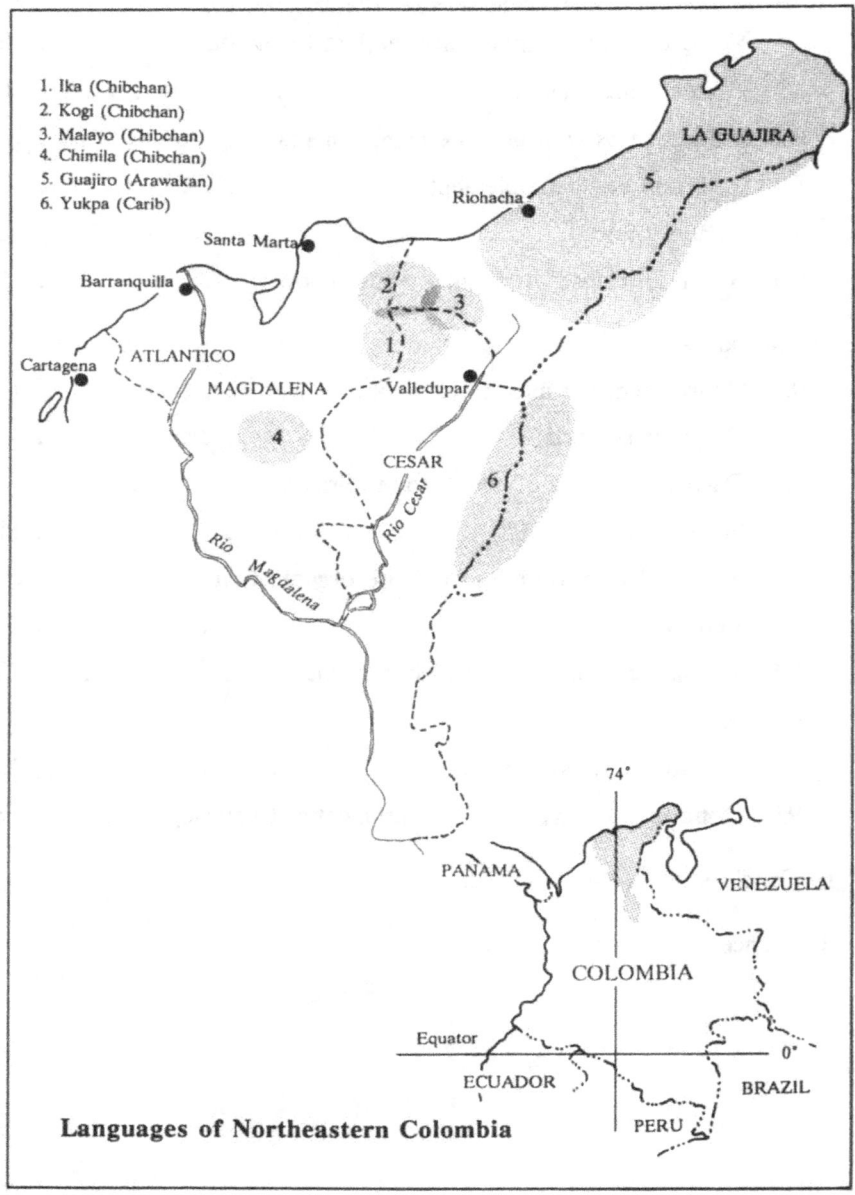

Foreword

Colombia, land of El Dorado, land of gold and emeralds! But even more precious are the gems found—not beneath its soil—but within its indigenous languages. Among these gems I would count the auxiliary verb system of Kogi, the positional verbs of Ika, the compound verbs of Epena, the evidential systems of Tucanoan languages, as well as their noun classifier systems.

For ten weeks in the fall of 1984, it was my privilege to lead a workshop, guiding several SIL colleagues in writing grammar sketches from a typological and functional perspective. What began as mere 'sketches' have become valuable grammars, and now with the publication of the first of these, we must acknowledge the authors' success.

The following impress me as the most significant reasons why this project yielded such rich fruit:

1. The typological/functional perspective provided an excellent framework for writing—as was our intention—broad, useful, descriptive grammars. Linguists and nonlinguists alike should be able to derive from them an accurate and fairly complete picture of what these languages are like, without the prerequisites that a more theoretical approach would have demanded.

2. All of the participants brought to the workshop an extensive knowledge of the language, acquired through months or years of study, and (with some exceptions) an exhaustive morpheme concordance of texts collected in their fieldwork. These slip concordances served as sources of examples, insights, and challenging 'residue'. And each participant brought

a terrific amount of energy, expended in long hours writing drafts at a very arduous pace.

3. At the beginning of the workshop, the authors were given a very general outline, and for each language, the corresponding files (empty except for the headings) were created on the disk in the computer center. The authors worked 'on-line', adding descriptive text and examples under the various headings, all the while refining and modifying the initial outline to fit the structure of the language being described. Consequently, there is some commonality to the structure of the various grammars, but without the negative effects of 'squeezing' the descriptions into a fixed, predetermined outline. (Mark Nelson and Bob Reed made the environment for working on-line very congenial.)

4. In addition to writing grammars, Paul Frank and Grace Hensarling served as consultants in training to other authors. Other linguists contributed occasional suggestions, most worthy of mention being Janet Barnes, Terry Malone, and Bob Reed.

5. At the end of the workshop, there were drafts of most sections of the grammars. Obviously, a terrific amount of work has been done since that time to bring these up to their current form. The person most responsible for keeping alive the vision of seeing them finished and published is Paul Frank; without his carrying the torch, they might never have seen the light of day.

6. Finally, if these grammars are a source of delight, it is because the languages they describe are marvelous objects, reflecting the creativity both of the One who gave language to Man and of the speakers who—in using language—continually shape it to serve their purposes in their environment.

David Weber

Abbreviations

1	first-person singular	IMPF	imperfective
2	second-person singular	INCEP	inceptive
3	third-person singular	INT	intentive
1p	first-person plural	LIM	limitative
2p	second-person plural	LOC	locative
3p	third-person plural	MED	medial
12p	first- or second-person plural	NEG	negative
		NOM	nominalizer
3D	three dimensional noun class indicator	O	object
		OBL	obligation
ABLE	ability	PERI	peripheral participant
AUX	auxiliary verb	PN	pronoun
BEN	benefactive	PRF	perfect
CAUS	causative	PROH	prohibition
CERT	certainty	PROX	proximal
CF	comparative	PURP	purpose
CNT	contrary to expectation	Q	interrogative
COND	condition	RECIP	reciprocal or reflexive
COP	copula	REF	point of reference
DIST	distal	RES	result
EMPH	emphatic	RPT	reportative
ERG	ergative	S	subject
FOC	focus	TOP	topic
FUT	future	WIT	witness
GEN	genitive	x	exclusive person
IMM	immediate succession	?	meaning unknown
IMPER	impersonal		

Introduction

1.1. The genetic classification of the Ika language. Ika is a Chibchan language spoken by the Bíntukwa, approximately 7000 people living on the southern slopes of the Sierra Nevada de Santa Marta in northeastern Colombia.[1] Kogi, Malayo, and Chimila, which are also spoken in or near the Sierra Nevada de Santa Marta, are the languages most closely related to Ika. Although most sources place Ika within the Chibchan language family proper, Shafer (1962) posits a family coordinate with Chibchan, called Aruakan, consisting of Ika and its three sister languages.[2]

1.2. The Bíntukwa people. The Bíntukwa are an agricultural people; they grow corn, coffee, bananas, sugarcane, cassava, potatoes, onions, and avocados at elevations of between one and ten thousand feet. They also raise a small number of cattle, sheep, and goats and use oxen, horses, and mules for transport. Brown sugar, coffee, and avocados serve as cash crops. The people live in family groups near their fields, moving from field to field to plant, care for, and harvest their crops. Many families also maintain houses in villages, which serve as social and ceremonial centers.

---

[1] At this time, the stated preference of the community is for the people to be called the Bíntukwa (although the name Arhuaco is more commonly used) and the language Ika. The Bíntukwa have also been referred to as the Aruak, Arhuak, Ica, Ijca, Bintucua, or Vintukua.

[2] See also Constenla 1981; Jijón y Caamaño 1943; Key 1979; Loukotka 1935, 1938, 1968; Mason 1950; McQuown 1955; Rivet and Loukotka 1952; Tovar 1961; Wheeler 1972.

A central figure in Bíntukwa life is the *mami* or shaman. He serves as the intermediary between the people and the spirit world. The people consult him on all occasions of importance: marriage, birth, illness, death, naming of children, passage into adulthood, harvesting the first of the crops. The *mami* also serves as a bearer of knowledge of ritual, history, and beliefs—a cultural resource that may indeed be dwindling; it is said that few young men are now training for the role of *mami*.

There are political leaders among the Bíntukwa, both on the village level and for the group as a whole. The most respected *mami*s choose a governor *(cabildo gobernador)* who heads a small group of men known as the governing council *(junta directiva)*. The governing council represents the community in its dealings with the Colombian government and other outside groups and makes decisions pertaining to the community as a whole. The council and representatives from all areas of the community meet yearly to discuss and make decisions concerning important issues. These meetings take place in Nabusímake (formerly known as San Sebastián) and have frequently attracted Colombian government officials as well as politicans aspiring to public office.

The Bíntukwa live within a land reserve granted by the Colombian government to the indigenous peoples of the *Sierra Nevada de Santa Marta*. Nevertheless, the people face pressure from nonindigenous colonists who own land within the reserve, some for many years. The tensions between indigenous communities and colonist have increased and now the communities are buying back land as they are able, with the help of the Colombian government. Nonlocal control of schools among the Bíntukwa has also been a source of tension in recent years, but the Bíntukwa leadership now controls all local schooling and, in conjunction with government agencies, is developing a bilingual education program.

1.3. The source of data for this study. The data used in this study come from texts gathered by Hubert Tracy between 1968 and 1980 and from my own fieldwork with the Bíntukwa, undertaken between May and December 1984. The text collection includes narratives (primarily hunting stories), descriptions of animals and their habits, procedural texts (e.g., how to make clothing), conversations, explanations of customs, and some folktales. All of these materials were collected in semiformal sessions with native speakers of Ika. To supplement these materials, particularly with regard to infrequently occurring constructions and paradigms, I elicited additional data, primarily from Mr. Abrán Izquierdo Solís.

1.4–14 The typological characteristics of Ika

Ika is an sov language, as shown by the typological features discussed in the sections which follow.

1.4. Word order. The basic word order in main, declarative clauses in Ika is SOV, as seen in (1) and (2).

(1)   S   O   V
      José guiadžina wasa-na
      José puma   chase-DIST
      José went after a puma.

(2)   S   O   V
      iʔmʌni Juansitu keina -ki   guiadžina tšiwa g-ʌn   nuʔ-na
      once   Juancito place LOC   puma   goat   eat-IMPF AUX-DIST
      One time a puma killed a goat near Juancito's place.

1.5. Adpositions. Ika uses postpositions in adpositional phrases. Examples (3)–(5) illustrate the postpositions *-sin* 'with', *pari* 'from', and *-ikin* (limitative), respectively.

(3)   *[peri -sin]* *keiwi*   *zoža-na-rua*
      dog with   right^away go-DIST-1S
      I went with my dog.

(4)   *[emi pari]* *guiadžina* *zag-ʌn*   *nuʔ-na*
      here from   puma   steal-IMPF AUX-DIST
      A puma was stealing from here.

(5)   *eim -eki pari -ri žóu-kitši zʌnʔ waʔkʌ-zar -i*
      that LOC   from TOP all-EMPH   just   see-be   while

      [awión   waʔnʌ-ž -éki -kin]
      airplane fall-MED LOC LIM
      From there, you could see everything, as far as the airport (where the airplanes fall).

1.6. Head noun and adjective. Adjectives follow the head noun in the noun phrase, as in (6).

(6) kakarón   aroma
     shotgun^shell empty
     empty shotgun shell

In this respect, Ika does not fit the pattern of typical OV languages (Lehmann 1972, 1978) which usually show the order adjective-noun. It is not uncommon, however, for SOV languages to show the order noun-adjective.[3] Quantifiers also usually follow the head noun, as in (7).

(7) peri mouga
     dog   two
     two dogs

1.7. Head noun and genitive. Genitives generally precede the head noun. A genitive construction is made up of a possessor phrase and the head noun (the possessed item). The possessor phrase consists of a noun followed by *zei* (genitive). It is this possessor phrase, then, that usually precedes, but may follow, the head noun. In the following examples, the possessor phrase is bracketed; the genitive precedes the head noun in (8), and follows it in (9).

(8) [nivi zei] tutusoma
      1p   GEN   hat
     our hats

(9) tšinu [inʔgui zei]
     pig   one   GEN
     someone's pig

1.8. Affixation. Both prefixes and suffixes occur in Ika, although suffixes predominate. There is very little noun morphology. A noun or noun phrase may take case marking enclitics, e.g., *kaʔ-seʔ* (ground-locative) 'on the ground', *-ri* (topic), and person prefixes for kinship terms. Verb morphology, however, is more extensive. There are prefixes to indicate subject and object, but the majority of the affixes in the verb phrase are suffixes. These fall into four main classes: aspectual, modal, clause-connecting, and derivational suffixes. Examples (10)–(13) illustrate these four classes of verb suffixes, respectively.

---

[3]See for example the list of languages in Greenberg 1966, appendix II, where fifty-five percent of the sixty-four SOV languages have adjectives following the noun.

(10) ASPECTUAL
zož-ʌn
go-IMPF
going

(11) MODAL
nak-ikua
come-OBL
must come

(12) CLAUSE-CONNECTING
kʌtšar -eʔ
arrive then
he arrived and then...

(13) DERIVATIONAL
nik-ami
to^work-NOM
work

1.9. Relative clauses. A relative clause normally follows its noun head. Since case endings occur following the relative clause rather than being postposed directly to the noun, relative clauses are probably best treated as having an internal head. Example (14) illustrates a relative clause whose internal head is the subject of the restricting clause. The head noun of the relative clause is in bold and the clause itself is bracketed. Note the ergative ending -seʔ at the end of the embedded clause rather than on the head noun *iki inʔgui* 'a man' itself.

(14) *[iki inʔgui Rísiu zaʔki nuk-ža]* -seʔ -ri ʌn-tšua-na
man one Lisio name COP-MED ERG TOP REF-see-DIST
A man named Lisio saw it.

A relative clause may also occur preceding the noun head but instances are rare in my data. In (15), the relative clause modifies the following noun 'goat'.

(15) *[guiadžina -seʔ ga-na tšiwa]* -ri wanak-akí nuk-ž -abaʔ
puma ERG eat-DIST goat TOP bring-PRF AUX-MED LOC
where they had just brought the goat that the puma ate

A relative clause following its noun head is consistent with an adjective following its noun in Ika although the relative clause preceding a noun is more typical of an OV language.

1.10. Comparatives. In comparative constructions, the comparative adjective follows the standard of comparison, as in (16).

(16)   STANDARD   ADJECTIVE
      Pedru nʌʔʌn-guasi ingumʌ́n kawa ni
      Pedro 1-CF   more   seem   CERT
      Pedro is bigger than I.

1.11. Negation. Negation is marked in the verb phrase by the verb suffix *-uʔ* (negative), as in (17).

(17)   *eima   kusari   an-a-g-uʔ   nʌn-na   ni*
      that   deer   REF-12pS-eat-NEG   AUX-DIST   CERT
      We did not eat that deer.

1.12. Questions. In yes/no questions, the question marker occurs at the end of the sentence, as in (18).

(18)   *Jordán   nʌ-kuʌ-ža   no*
      Jordán   2S-live-MED   Q
      Do you live in Jordán?

In information questions, the question word is generally placed at the beginning of a sentence[4] while the question marker (*-o, -e,* or *no*) still appears at the end.

(19)   *beki   ás-ik-o*
      where   sit-OBL-Q
      Where shall I sit?

---

[4]Although question words almost always occur at the beginning of a clause, there is no evidence that this position is the result of movement. I have found no examples of questions where a question word refers to an object and is followed by a full noun phrase subject. In interrogative transitive clauses questioning an object, the subject is given information and not overtly referenced in the clause by a noun or pronoun. The question word thus appears in initial position simply because the subject is not present.

The next two examples question subject and object, respectively, and also have the question word sentence initially and the interrogative suffix sentence finally.

(20)   *ini*   *-ri*   *nai-n*   *nuk-ʌw-an-o*
      what?   TOP   walk-IMPF   AUX-AUX-IMPF-Q
      What could be walking?

(21)   *ini*   *was*   *-i*   *-ri*   *ei*   *ž-ʌn*   *no*
      what? chase while TOP thus say-IMPF Q
      What is it chasing, barking like that?

1.13. Coding of major syntactic functions. The major categories subject and object are primarily distinguished by differential marking on the verb. The single participant of an intransitive verb and the agent of a transitive verb are both referenced by the same verb-marking morphology. The intransitive verb in (22) and the transitive verb in (23) are both marked for first person by *-rua*.

(22)   *zoža-na-rua*
      go-DIST-1S
      I went.

(23)   *mi-tšua-na-rua*
      2O-see-DIST-1S
      I saw you.

A set of object prefixes serves several functions, the most basic of which is to reference a patient in a transitive verb or an indirect object of a bitransitive verb (e.g., give, sell, buy). (23) illustrates the second-person-object prefix *mi-*, and (24) shows that, when subject and object prefixes both occur, the subject prefix precedes the object prefix.

(24)   *nʌ-nive-ʔzasana*   *u-ž-e*
      2S-1pO-pay   AUX-MED-Q
      Did you pay us?

There is no separate indirect object category. With bitransitive verbs, the recipient of the object is referenced by the object prefix. The second-person indirect object of (25) is thus marked in verb morphology in the same way as the second-person object of (26), by *mi-* (second-person-object).

(25) *mi-k-ʌngei?-na-rua*
      2O-PERI-sell-DIST-1S
      I sold it to you.

(26) *mi-tšua   u-ž-in*
      2O-see   AUX-MED-WIT
      He saw you.

Subject noun phrases usually precede the object in linear order.

1.14. Ergativity. Ika is basically a nominative-accusative language in both verb morphology and syntactic phenomena but evidences two types of split ergativity—differential marking of the single participant of intransitive verbs in verb morphology and optional case marking of transitive subject noun phrases.

As indicated verb morphology is essentially nominative-accusative, with the same person-marking affixes referencing both the agent of transitive verbs and the single participant of intransitive verbs. Syntactic phenomena also show a nominative-accusative pattern. With imperatives, for example, neither the agent of transitive nor subject of intransitive is stated. More significantly, verbal complementation usually involves some sort of same-subject/different-subject restriction associating the transitive agent and intransitive subject. Adverbial clauses expressing simultaneous action, for example, must have the same subject as the verb of the main clause in which the adverbial is embedded. Thus, in (27) both *was* 'chase' and *žun* 'go down' must have the same subject, in nominative-accusative alignment, even though the agent of 'chase' is ergative-marked (as will be discussed shortly).

(27) *peri -se? -ri   win-was -i   žun-na*
      dog   ERG   TOP   3pS-chase while   go^down-DIST
      The dogs went down chasing it.

The vast majority of verb roots in Ika take standard subject marking for both the agent of a transitive verb and the single participant of an intransitive verb, but one small group of intransitive verbs always references the single participant by object prefixes in an ergative-absolutive pattern. This small set of intransitive verbs can be characterized semantically as referencing a participant as an EXPERIENCER. (28) illustrates a clause with a transitive verb, in which there is a first-person object referenced on the verb by the prefix *nʌ-*. The verb *a?tikuma* 'forget' in (29) uses the same prefix to reference the single participant of the verb.

(28) nʌ-tsua-na
     1O-see-DIST
     He saw me.

(29) na-ʔtikuma-na
     1O-forget-DIST
     I forgot.

Dixon (1979:84) has called this sort of split ergativity SPLIT S-MARKING, a cover term for cases "where intransitive verbs fall into two mutually exclusive subclasses, one using A[gent]-marking and the other O[bject]-marking for its S[ubject] NP," with subclasses based on the semantic type of the verb. That is, an intransitive verb that marks a transitive agent involves a volitional agent in control of an action, whereas a verb that marks a transitive patient is one that involves a nonvolitional agent not in control of the action.

A survey of this type of verb (§2.6) shows this same semantic basis for verbs that take object marking. Dixon states that the size of the class of intransitive verbs taking what he calls O-marking varies from language to language, from being a large open class in some languages to being a small class of only a few dozen verbs in other languages. Indeed, Ika is at the end of the spectrum having only a small number of such verbs. Because of the rarity of verbs which show this ergative-absolutive pattern of person marking in the verb morphology, I have chosen to present the person marking affixes as subject and object markers. Since the Chibchan languages of Central America are basically ergative in nature (Constenla 1982 and personal communication), this aspect of split ergativity in Ika may be a remnant of what was formerly an essentially ergative system.

The other aspect of split ergativity in Ika involves the differential marking of agent noun phrases in transitive clauses. Overt noun phrase references to agents in transitive clauses may be marked by -seʔ (ergative), as seen in (30).

(30) tigri   -seʔ   tšinu kʌ-ga-na
     jaguar   ERG   pig   PERI-eat-DIST
     A jaguar ate his pig.

The subject of intransitive clauses and the object in transitive clauses receive no case marking. This ergative case marking is optional in the sense that it does not appear on every agent noun phrase and is not categorically controlled by some factor such as an animacy hierarchy, as discussed by Silverstein (1976) and others. Essentially, the agent noun phrase is marked by *-se?* whenever it occurs contiguous to the verb (i.e., not in its canonical position before the object (see §9.3). Dixon (1979:89) notes that "in most examples of split conditioned by the semantic nature of verbs, bound affixes are involved; whereas, in most examples of split conditioned by the semantic nature of NPs, case marking is involved." Ika partially follows this pattern in that the split evidenced in verb morphology depends on the semantic nature of intransitive verbs, although the split evidenced in case marking is based not so much on the semantic nature of noun phrases as on word order.

1.15. Ika phonology. Ika phonemes[5] are presented in (31) and (32). Symbols in parentheses indicate how the associated phoneme is written in this study.

Stress usually falls on the penultimate syllable and is marked here only when any other syllable is stressed in polysyllabic words.

(31)   Ika consonants

		Bilabial	Alveolar	Alveopalatal	Velar	Glottal
Stop	vl	p	t		k	ʔ
	vd	b	d		g	
Fricative	vl		s			h
	vd	β(w)	z	ž		
Affricate	vl			tš		
	vd			dž		
Flap			r			
Nasal		m	n(n,ŋ)			

---

[5]See Tracy and Tracy 1973 for details on Ika phonology. In a few words, the velar nasal (ŋ) appears to contrast with *n* prevocalically, e.g., *aruŋʌn* 'think' vs. *drunʌn* 'fly'. For this reason, Tracy and Tracy 1973 lists the velar nasal as a separate phoneme. The syllable boundary, however, always follows any intervocalic ŋ. It could thus be said that the phoneme *n* is realized as a velar nasal syllable finally before vowels, before velar consonants, and word finally. In this work, however, intervocalic *n* with a velar articulation is written ŋ for the sake of clarity. The vowel ʌ presented problems in the original analysis, and its representation in the practical orthography has lead to confusion. ʌ occurs almost exclusively in closed syllables (with some instances of variation between *a* and ʌ in unstressed open syllables), but neither *a* nor *i* occurs in closed syllables. Using morphological clues, it is possible to identify alternation between *a* and ʌ and between *i* and ʌ, as described in the section on morphophonemics. The Bíntukwa community has apparently decided to group ʌ and *i* as one element in the orthography, as distinct from *a*. I have taken the approach of maintaining ʌ as a separate element in this work because of uncertainties concerning its phonemic status.

(32) Ika vowels

	Front	Central	Back
High	i	ɨ	u
Mid	e	ʌ	o
Low		a	

Diphthongs are composed of a nonsyllabic *i* or *u* plus another vowel, as indicated in (33). In the combination *ui*, it is *u* which is nonsyllabic.

(33) Ika diphthongs

u/i onglide	u/i offglide
ua	ei
uɨ	ou
iɨ	
ui	
ue	
uʌ	

Ika syllable structure involves simple or diphthongal syllable nuclei with optional onset and coda. (The examples in this section do not show morpheme boundaries; a period indicates syllable division.) A simple syllable onset may be any consonant except glottal stop. A complex onset may be made up of a stop plus *r*.

(34) Syllable onset

Simple	Complex
CV	CCV.CVC
ma	dru.nʌn
you	fly

Syllables may be either open or closed. A simple syllable coda may be any consonant except the voiced fricatives; glottal stop occurs only as a syllable coda. Stops and *s*, however, may close a syllable only when immediately followed by an identical segment. The only allowable complex coda is *nʔ*.

(35) Syllable coda

Simple	Complex	Stop or s
VC.CVC.CVVC.CV	V.CVCC	CVC.CVV
ʌm.win.guaʔ.na	a.wʌnʔ	tšuk.kui
they killed it	big	rat

1.16-19 Ika morphophonemics

Morphophonemic alternations in Ika can be divided into four types: (a) alternations which can be understood in terms of rules of phoneme combination, (b) alternations of one segment with another which are regular yet not required by rules of phoneme combination, (c) alternations of vowels and ∅ governed by syllable structure patterns, and (d) morphophonemic fusion.

The first group (§1.16) involves changes governed strictly by phonological principles. These alternations change nonallowable phoneme combinations into allowable combinations. Because no alternation can be said to have occurred without reference to underlying forms of morphemes, I have included these alternations under morphophonemics rather than phonemics. The second group (§1.17) involves automatic alternations which apply only at morpheme boundaries, changing one possible or allowable phoneme combination into another. The third group (§1.18) deals with underlying cv patterns of morphemes and the way these patterns govern vowel/∅ alternations at morpheme boundaries. The fourth group (§1.19) describes changes in which segments fuse to form a third segment.

1.16. Phonologically conditioned variation. The following paragraphs describe alternations directly related to patterns of phoneme combination.

A nasal and following obstruent always share the same point of articulation; consequently *n* becomes *m* before bilabials. Compare the forms of ʌn- (point of reference) in (36) and (37).

(36) ʌn-tšua
 REF-see
 see it

(37) ʌm-win-guak
 REF-3pS-kill
 they kill it

r becomes *d* following a nasal. Compare the forms of -*ri* (topic) in (38) and (39).

Ika

(38) *Dorori   -ri*
     Dolores   TOP

(39) *Sʌwʌstian -di*
     Sebastian TOP

Low vowels *e, a, o* are raised to *i, ʌ, u*, respectively, in closed syllables. Compare the forms of *itšon* 'go up', *nan* 'be', and *aʔtšugen* 'collide' below. (Syllable division rather than morpheme boundaries are indicated in these examples.)

(40) V.CV.CVC.CVC.CV
     i.tšo.nʌm.pʌn.na
     he began to go up

(41) V.CVC.CV
     i.tšun.na
     he went up

(42) CV.CV
     na.reʔ
     was, and then . . .

(43) CVC.CV
     nʌn.na
     was

(44) VC.CV.CV.CVC
     aʔ.tšu.ge.nʌn
     colliding

(45) VC.CV.CVC.CV
     aʔ.tšu.gin.na
     collided

The mid central vowel ʌ never occurs word finally but is raised to i in that position.[6] (46) and (47) illustrate this raising in the word *iki* 'people'.

(46) *ikʌ   -zei*
     people GEN
     of the people

(47) *iki*
     people

1.17. Alternations applying only at morpheme boundaries. Several other morphophonemic alternations are regular but not governed by patterns of phoneme combination. Even though the sequences *ki/ke* and *ni/ne* occur within morphemes, *k* becomes *s* and *n* becomes *r* when followed by a front vowel across a morpheme boundary. The word *neki* 'contrary to expectation', for example, shows both *n* and *k* followed by front vowels, yet these same consonants change when followed by front vowels across a morpheme boundary. The following examples illustrate these changes with the *k* of *nuk* and the final *n* of *nan* (copular/auxiliary verbs). The first word in each set illustrates the basic form of each verb, when not followed by a front vowel.

(48) *nuk-ikua*   *nus-eʔ*   *nus-i*
      be-OBL   be-then   be-while

(49) *nan-uʔ*   *nar-eʔ*   *nar-i*
      be-NEG   be-then   be-while

Morpheme-final *k* becomes glottal stop before a consonant. This change occurs even before *k* although the sequence *kk* does occur within a morpheme in words such as *tšukkui* 'rat'. Morpheme-final *k* changes to glottal stop before a consonant across a morpheme boundary even when

---

[6]The ʌ/i alternation could be seen as a lowering process, thus making the citation form of the word the basic form. Spanish loan words, however, show a similar raising of mid to high vowels word finally, e.g., *puenti* 'bridge' (Spanish *puente*) and *kʌbažu* 'horse' (Spanish *caballo*). If ʌ and i are treated as a single phoneme, however, this raising would be described as an allophonic process rather than as a morphophonemic one.

that consonant is another k.[7] (50) and (51) illustrate this change in the verb root *nak* 'come'.

(50) nak-ʌm-pʌn-na
come-IMPF-INCEP-DIST
began to come

(51) naʔ-na
come-DIST
came

The sequences *iʔ* and *ʌʔ* occur within morphemes as in the words *ziʔ* 'red' and *nʌʔʌn* (first singular pronoun), but *i* and *ʌ* are lowered to *e* and *a*, respectively, when preceding a glottal stop across a morpheme boundary. Consider the final vowels in the object prefixes *nivi-* (first plural object) and *nʌ-* (first singular object) when they occur before *ʔzasana* 'pay'.

(52) nive-ʔzasana   u-ž-in
1pO-pay   AUX-MED-WIT
He paid us.

(53) na-ʔzasana   u-ž-in
1O-pay   AUX-MED-WIT
He paid me.

1.18. Vowel/∅ alternations. Many morphemes, both roots and affixes, show two variants—one with and one without an extra vowel at the morpheme boundary. For example, compare the form of *nak* 'come' in *naʔ-na* (come-DIST) 'came' with its uninflected form in (54).

(54) naka   u-ž-in
come   AUX-MED-WIT
He came.

Consider, also, the forms of *-na* (distal) below where this morpheme appears (a) word finally, (b) before a vowel-initial suffix, and (c) before a consonant-initial suffix.

---

[7]The phonetic difference between *kk* and *ʔk* is slight, but one clue to distinguishing the two is that most vowels have a shorter and more lax allophone before *kk*.

(55) naʔ-na
      come-DIST
      he came

(56) naʔ-n   -ameʔ
      come-DIST   CAUS
      because he came

(57) naʔ-na   -ri
      come-DIST   TOP
      he came

It might seem that these morphophonemic alternations represent either epenthesis or vowel deletion. Yet consider the different behavior of -*ku* (medial) and -*ikua* (obligation) in (58) and (59).

(58) naʔ-ku-in
      come-MED-WIT
      I came

(59) nak-ikua
      come-OBL
      must come

-*ikua* occurs without initial *i* following a vowel-final morpheme, yet with the *i* after a consonant. If *i* represented an epenthetic vowel, it should also occur between *nak* and -*ku* (medial). Since it does not, I do not believe that the presence or absence of the vowel should be treated as epenthesis.

There are two problems with describing this vowel/∅ alternation as deletion. First, it makes sense to delete one of two vowels coming together across a morpheme boundary, but it seems unusual to delete a vowel between consonants. For example, if the basic form of 'come' is *naka* and the shorter form in *naʔ-na* (come-DIST) 'came' results from deleting the final *a*, then one must assume that some vowels are deleted adjacent to a vowel (across the morpheme boundary) while others are deleted before either a vowel or a consonant.

Second, a deletion analysis forces the problematic matter of determining which vowel to delete, the first or the second. Example (60) and (61) contrast two cases involving vowel 'deletion' where the outcome is different under apparently identical circumstances. The second line of each example gives the longer form of each morpheme as its basic form. In both cases, *a* is followed by *e*, but in (60) the *a* is deleted while in (61) the *e* is deleted. This suggests that the vowel/∅ alternation is a property of particular morphemes, not the result of a deletion rule.

(60) zoža-n -ekɨ
    zoža-na -ekɨ
    go-DIST LOC
    where he went

(61) keina -kɨ
    keina -ekɨ
    place LOC
    someone's home

A more accurate characterization of these alternations might be that each morpheme's underlying form specifies a constant CV pattern or syllable structure in addition to particular segments that realize this structure. For instance, the underlying form of the locative suffix in (60) and (61) would be as in (62). The *e* in parentheses indicates that if the preceding morpheme does not end in a vowel, the locative suffix supplies *e* in order to maintain its VCV shape; otherwise the *e* does not appear in the surface form of the morpheme.

(62) V C V
     (e) k ɨ

The suffix *-na* (distal) would be handled differently. The underlying form of this suffix would be as in (63). When no vowel immediately follows the suffix, a general rule would supply *a*.

(63) C V
      n

I have two reasons for proposing this analysis. First of all, *a* is by far the most frequent vowel involved in vowel/∅ alternations. Secondly, whenever *a* and a different vowel come together across a morpheme boundary, *a* is usually deleted regardless of its position in the sequence. By positing an empty vowel in the underlying form, it is possible to state a general rule supplying most of the optional vowels, without a need for a separate rule specifying which vowel is realized in a sequence of two optional vowels.

It is not my purpose here to give a complete analysis of vowel/∅ alternations, but I believe that such an analysis should be developed along the lines sketched above.

1.19. Morphophonemic fusion. There is one instance of two segments fusing to form a third segment: when *k* is followed by *ž*, the two fuse to form *g*.[8] Consider the following. When followed by *-e?* 'then', the verb roots *nik* 'work' and *nuk* 'be' become *nise?* and *nuse?*. The fact that the verb-root-final *k* becomes *s* before *e*, as described above, indicates that *-e?* immediately follows the verb root. If *-ž* (medial) occurs between one of these roots and *-e?*, however, the results are *nige?* and *nuge?*, respectively, *k* and *ž* fusing to form *g*. This fusion takes place in all cases where morphemes ending in *k* are followed by *ž*. In words such as these, there is no longer any segment which uniquely represents (medial) since the *g* belongs to both the root and the suffix. I write words in which this fusion occurs, however, as in (64), even though *g* occurs phonemically rather than *kž*.

(64)   *nik-ž*   *-e?*
       do-MED   then

Some forms show evidence of two vowels or a vowel and a glide having collapsed together, although a third, distinct segment does not result, as in the case of *k* and *ž*. The auxiliary verb *u*, for example, has two morphophonemic alternants, *u* before consonant-initial suffixes and *aw* before vowel-initial suffixes. Thus, *aw* is chosen before *-u?* (negative), but the resulting form is *au?*, with *w* and *u* collapsing to *u*. *w* is also lost before *o*, in *ás-iku̯-o* (sit-must-interrogative), which becomes *ásiko* 'where should I sit?' Another case of the collapsing of vowels is the combination ʌ*nkari* 'converse' and *-i* 'while' as ʌ*nkarí*. In cases of two identical vowels in sequence, they collapse to one, with word stress often shifting to that vowel.

---

[8]Ika *ž* derives historically from *i and there is comparative evidence that, at least in some circumstances, *k* became *g* before *i* (Bob Jackson, personal communication). Thus, the pattern described here probably reflects that historical process.

2
Word Classes in Ika

The major word classes in Ika include nouns, adjectives, and verbs, each of which, in turn, may be subdivided further. Among the minor classes are adverbs, personal pronouns, demonstrative pronouns, postpositions, conjunctions, noun adjuncts, and verb adjuncts. This chapter briefly discusses each of these categories and notes the sections where particular topics are covered in greater detail in later sections.

2.1. Nouns. Nouns may be divided into the following subclasses: kinship terms, proper names, nouns derived from verbs, and other nouns. Kinship terms carry person prefixes indicating whose kinsperson is being referred to, e.g., *nʌ-kaki* (first-father) 'my father'. When used as a term of address, a kinship term does not take a person prefix (e.g., *kaki* 'father'). Proper names are generally borrowed from Spanish with considerable assimilation to Ika phonological patterns.

Nouns derived from verbs do not appear to be very frequent. The nominalizer *-ami* can be seen in *nik-ami* (work-NOM) 'work'; *-ʌža* (nominalizer) derives a noun from a verb, with the meaning 'a person who characteristically does an action', e.g., *zág-ʌža* (steal-NOM) 'thief'.

2.2. Adjectives. A small number of adjectives by themselves may serve as noun modifiers or as predicate adjectives in descriptive clauses. The adjective *aroma* 'empty' falls into this class.

(65) tšokuɨ   aroma
      gourd^bowl   empty
      empty dish

Most adjectives must occur with *kawa* 'seem' (or another copula, see §2.9), both when modifying a noun and as a predicate adjective. In descriptive clauses with predicate adjectives, *kawa* serves as the verb.

(66) Juansitu   warin   kawa   ni
      Juancito   tall   seem   CERT
      Juancito is tall.

In noun phrases these adjectives plus *kawa* look something like relative clauses. In example (67), the adjective phrase *awʌnʔ kawa* (big seem) serves as a modifier in the noun phrase. The head noun is in bold and the adjective phrase is bracketed.

(67) **anáʔnuga**   [awʌnʔ kawa]   guákʌ-ža
      animal   big   seem   kill-MED
      It kills big animals.

2.3 – 2.10 Verbs

There are at least eight categories of verbs in Ika: intransitive, transitive, bitransitive, impersonal verbs, verbs that take a sentential object, quotation-like verbs, copulas, and auxiliary verbs.

2.3. Intransitive verbs. Intransitive verbs are one-participant verbs or, in the case of a motion verb, one participant plus optional location. Subject person affixes on an intransitive verb reference this single participant. The verb root *asa* 'sit down' is an intransitive verb.

(68) eim   -éki   -ri   win-asa   aw   -i   -ri
      there LOC   TOP   3pS-sit   AUX   while   TOP
      They are sitting down there,...

2.4. Transitive verbs. Transitive verbs involve two participants. Subject is referenced in a transitive verb by the same person affixes used to reference subject in intransitive verbs. Object is referenced by object prefixes (§5.2).

(69)   mi-tšua-na-rua
       2O-see-DIST-1S
       I saw you.

Subject noun phrases may be marked by *-seʔ* (ergative) (§9.3).

(70)   a   -seʔ -ri   du   tšua u-na
       3   ERG   TOP   well   see   AUX-DIST
       He looked it over well.

A transitive clause without ergative marking on the subject NP usually shows the standard SOV order with explicit reference to both subject and object.

(71)   Gʌriwieri tigri   aʔwasa-na
       Gabriel   jaguar   chase-DIST
       Gabriel hunted a jaguar.

2.5. Bitransitive verbs. Bitransitive verbs involve subject, object, and a source or goal for the movement of the object. Subject and object noun phrases are not marked for case; the human participant who is the source or goal is marked by *-seʔ*. A nonthird-person source/goal is referenced on the verb by an object prefix.

(72)   Abran -di   Juan -seʔ kafé   aʔbe   u-ž-in
       Abran TOP   Juan LOC   coffee   deliver AUX-MED-WIT
       Abran delivered coffee to Juan.

Ika has a series of bitransitive verbs meaning 'put down' which are used with objects of different shapes: long and thin (*gaka*), three dimensional (*sa*), flat (*pan*), and things with an upright orientation (*tšoʔs*). (73) and (74) demonstrate this contrast for *kʌn* 'stick' and *paperi* 'paper'. (See §5.3 for an explanation of the noun classes involved.)

(73)   kʌn   kaʔ   -seʔ   gakó   u
       stick   ground   LOC   putˆdown   AUX
       Put the stick on the ground!

(74)   paperi   kaʔ   -seʔ   pa   ú
       paper   ground   LOC   putˆdown   AUX
       Put the paper on the ground!

2.6. Impersonal verbs. Some verbs, e.g., *aʔzan* 'think, feel' and *kusein* 'get better', have only one participant referenced on the verb by an object-person prefix. Note the first-person object marker *nʌ-* in (75).

(75)   *nʌ-kusein-uʔ*   *gui*   *ni*
       1O-recover-NEG   also   CERT
       I still have not recovered.

This is essentially an ergative pattern, but the vast majority of verbs show nominative-accusative person-marking, with a small, closed set showing the pattern described here. This phenomenon is similar to what Givón (1984:143-44) calls dative subjects—experiencer subjects which are case marked as dative objects. It is also similar to some verbs in Latin, e.g., the verb for 'repent', for which the single participant occurs in the accusative.[9] I will use the term IMPERSONAL to capture the fact that the one participant is referenced by the object markers but there is no subject involved.[10] (76) lists the verbs which I have identified as impersonal verbs.

(76)   *aguntan*   'be tired'
       aʔsinkirin   'sneeze'
       aʔten   'be wet and cold'
       aʔtikuma   'forget'
       aʔzan   'think, feel'
       angakuma   'be, get frightened'
       gʌnkua   'know'
       gumʌtšan   'be drunk'
       kawa   'seem or have to x'
       kʌpʌŋa   'get sick'
       kʌzan   'be busy or occupied'
       kusein   'recover, get better'

2.7. Verbs with sentential objects. Two verbs which take sentential objects are *guaʔsa* 'cause' and *kawa* 'seem'. *guaʔsa* takes an object whose verb is marked only by *-ʌn* (imperfective); the subject of the embedded clause is not coreferential with the subject of *guaʔsa*.

---

[9]Adolfo Constenla helped clarify my thinking on impersonal verbs.
[10]See §1.14 for a fuller discussion of ergativity in Ika in relation to these verbs.

(77) *[ši   wis-ʌn]   neki gua?s-u?   nar -i*
     foul^odor spray^out-IMPF CNTR cause-NEG AUX while
     (She) did not let the skunk's scent spray out,...

kawa used with a sentential object unmarked for mood is interpreted as 'it seems that *x*'.

(78) *[mákʌri -se? ga-na]   kaw-in*
     vulture ERG eat-DIST seem-WIT
     It seems that a vulture ate it.

2.8. Quotation-like verbs. A number of verbs involving speech, perception, or cognition take a sentential complement which is a full clause with an inflected, finite verb. Examples are *ža* 'say', *tšua* 'see', and *a?zan* 'think'.[11]

(79) *Pedru kʌ́nkʌnʌn nai-n   zei-kua nʌ-kʌ-ža-n   -ame?*
     Pedro forest   walk-IMPF go-OBL 1O-PERI-say-DIST because
     because Pedro Arias said to me, "Let's go hunting,"...

(80) *kusari džumena pa   na keiwi   tšua-na-rua*
     deer   unsought flat COP right^away see-DIST-1S
     I unexpectedly saw a deer lying down.

2.9. Copular verbs. The set of copular verbs includes *nan, zan, a?zan, zanik* 'become', and *kawa*. Descriptive clauses (with an adjectival complement) use all of these copular verbs, depending on the particular adjective involved.

(81) *Juan kui?ma na ni*
     Juan young   COP CERT
     John is young.

(82) *ingi nʌ-kaw -ame?*
     little 1O-seem CAUS
     Because I am small,...

---

[11]Each of these verbs also fits in another class: *ža* and *tšua* with transitive verbs, and *a?zan* with impersonal verbs.

(83)   *meina -ri   ouró zar-in*
       gully TOP   deep COP-WIT
       The gully is deep.

(84)   *sinki ʌn-zanis   -i*
       late REF-became while
       getting late

(85)   *anei aʔzi-ni*
       tasty COP-CERT
       It is tasty.

Equative clauses (with a nominal complement) use *nan* as copula.

(86)   *Kažatani kʌbirdu na   ni*
       Cayetano cabildo COP CERT
       Cayetano is the cabildo [a political office].

nan is optional for statements true in the present.

(87)   *eima   guioma geirota   ni*
       this   snake   coral^snake   CERT
       This snake is a coral snake.

Clauses indicating location or position use both *nan* and *zan* as the copula.

(88)   *guiadžina -ri   ei   tšo   nar   -eʔ*
       puma   TOP   thus standing COP   then
       The puma was standing, ...

(89)   *ranta kuʌ-ž   -abaʔ guin zan -ʌndi*
       tapir live-MED   LOC   ?   COP COND
       If it is where the tapir lives, ...

2.10. Auxiliary verbs. The auxiliary verbs include *nan*, *nuk*, and *u*. *nan* is used following a verb with a negative or modal suffix. *nuk* occurs as an auxiliary verb with progressive and perfect tense-aspect. *u* is used for virtually all the remaining cases; it has two allomorphs—*u* before consonant-initial suffixes and *aw* before vowel-initial suffixes.[12]

2.11. Adverbs. The category ADVERB includes words that specify manner (*mʌni* 'rapidly', *keiwɨ* 'right away', *eigui* 'again', *eiki* 'still'), relative time words (*iwa* 'now, today', *sai* 'yesterday'), absolute time words (*džuikuʔ* 'noon', *sinkɨ* 'after sundown', probably from Spanish *las cinco* 'five o'clock'), days of the week borrowed from Spanish (*runibaʔ* 'Monday', *bierne* 'Friday'), and location words (*warekɨ* 'up high', *žʌkkɨ* 'over yonder', *wamɨsárigʌn* 'at the head of'). Additional relative time words are listed in (90).

(90) *sigeʔ* 'next day, tomorrow' *sai* 'yesterday'
      mougeʔ 'day after tomorrow' *muʔzɨne* 'two days ago'
      maieʔ 'in three days' *máizɨne* 'three days ago'
      maʔkaieʔ 'in four days'

One series of adverbs indicates the number of times an action is performed (*iʔmʌnɨ* 'one time', *múʔmuru* 'two times', *máimuru* 'three times', and *maʔkéimuru* 'four times'). Other adverbs modify adjectives, (*ingɨ diwʌ́n* (little different) 'a little bit different', *ingɨ mʌtšei* (little close) 'fairly close to', *guamɨ kɨ* 'less cold', *deh kɨ* 'very cold', and *ingumʌ́n diwʌ́n* (lot different) 'very different'). These adverbs always occur to the left of the adjective they modify.

Another element serving as an adverb is a phrase which compares how two actions are performed. Such an adverbial phrase is bracketed in (91).

(91) *[teréfono nar -i] tininin keiwɨ i -eʔ -ri*
      telephone be while ring right^away say then TOP
      It rang like a telephone does, . . .

2.12. Pronouns. Personal pronouns distinguish first, second, and third person, singular and plural. They occur infrequently in text—occasionally in subject position, very rarely in object position, and most frequently as the object of a postposition, as in *ma-sin* (second-with) 'with you' or *niwi zei* (first-plural genitive) 'our'. The six personal pronouns are presented in (92).

---

[12]§5.1 outlines the circumstances in which auxiliary verbs occur.

(92) nʌn   (first-person singular)
    ma   (second-person singular)
    a   (third-person singular)
    niwi   (first-person plural)
    miwi   (second-person plural)
    ikʌŋa? (third-person plural)

The infrequent pronoun *manʌnka?* is a first-person inclusive form (Hugh Tracy, personal communication)[13] whereas *niwi* is usually used exclusively. With the exception of third-person forms, personal pronouns are phonologically related to object prefixes (§5.2).

Demonstrative pronouns distinguish distance and deictic or anaphoric reference. The most common demonstrative pronouns are listed in (93). *ʌža* is used anaphorically while *eima* refers to something in the physical context.

(93) ʌža   'this or that one'   (anaphoric)
     eima   'this or that one'   (being pointed to)
     žama   'that one'   (choice among alternatives)
     žika   'that one there'   (alternative farther away)

eima and either *žama* or *žika* are used in contexts involving a choice between alternatives, as in (94). Using *žika* 'that one there' rather than *žama* would indicate that the second alternative is farther away than the first one.[14]

(94) bema   me-ʔdžun-o, kua eima   kua žama
     which^one?   2o-want-Q   or   this^one   or   that^one
     'Which one do you want, this one or that one?'

2.13. Noun adjuncts. Elements commonly found in noun phrases are quantifiers, articles, adjectives, and numerals. Noun phrases may also have case markers. Two quantifiers are *žou* 'all' and *imi* 'much'. Ika generally does not mark definiteness, but the demonstrative pronoun *eima* 'this,

---

[13]Landaburu 1985 mentions that *manʌnka?* is sometimes used as an indirect form for 'you' in reference to the defendent in trials.

[14]Interrogative pronouns, used in content questions, are discussed in §6.2.

that' may be used to indicate definiteness. Further, the numeral *in?gui* 'one' is at times used to indicate indefiniteness. Finally, the topic marker *-ri* is commonly found on noun phrases.

Ika numerals are based upon a decimal system. There are single words for one to nine and phrases for the numbers ten to ninety-nine. A numeral phrase names a number of tens first, followed by a number of ones.

(95) *mouga   uga   in?gui   kʌttou*
       two   tens   one   ones
       twenty-one

By borrowing Spanish numerals (*sientu* 'hundred'), it is possible to compose numbers above one hundred, but the Spanish system is generally coming to be used more than the native Ika system.[15]

2.14. Verb adjuncts. Among the elements found in the verb phrase are main verbs, auxiliary verbs, adverbs, and verb affixes. Verb affixes include person-marking prefixes and suffixes (both subject and object), the negative suffix, modal suffixes, temporal-aspect suffixes, deictic suffixes, clause connecting suffixes (indicating subordinating or coordinating relationships), and mood markers.[16]

2.15. Conjunctions. There are few conjunctions. Adjectives and nouns are conjoined only by *sin* 'with', *sin* marking the second item in a conjoined phrase. Clauses are conjoined by means of clause-connecting suffixes in the verb phrase, optionally followed by one of three clause-combining conjunctions—*pari* 'from that point', *guinti* 'finally', or *nʌngua* 'and'.

2.16. Postpositions. Postpositions in Ika serve at least two functions—case marking (ergative, locative, genitive, indirect object, limitative, instrument, accompaniment), locational or positional relationships ('under', 'from'). Some postpositions are independent, stress-bearing words, but most postpositions are enclitic. At least one, *zʌ* (genitive), is at times proclitic.[17]

---

[15]Noun adjuncts are discussed further in §3; case marking is discussed in §4.

[16]Most verb adjuncts are discussed further in §5; clause connecting suffixes and mood markers are discussed in §7.

[17]See §4 for more detail on postpositions.

3
The Noun Phrase

This chapter summarizes the roles of quantifiers, numerals, adjectives, articles, casemarking, and nouns used attributively.[18]

3.1. Quantifiers. Quantifiers follow the head noun in noun phrases. Ika quantifiers are listed in (96).

(96) *džina*   'plural'
     imɨ   'many, much'
     ingɨ   'a little'
     reʔmasi 'many' (used only with animate objects)
     sʌmmɨ   'much' (used only with inanimate objects)
     žou   'all'

Examples of quantifiers are *džua ingɨ* (blood little) 'a little blood', *perɨ imɨ* (dog many) 'many dogs', *urakɨ žou* (house all) 'all the houses', *akunsi sʌmmɨ* (cooked^food much) 'much cooked food', and *ikɨ reʔmasi* (person many) 'many people'. Nouns are not marked as singular or plural, but the quantifier *džina* (plural) conveys the idea of 'more than one' without specifying any absolute or relative quantity, as in *nʌ-gunamɨ džina* (first-worker plural) 'my workers'.

---

[18]§2.12 summarizes personal and demonstrative pronouns. §8.1 discusses relative clauses.

Another type of quantifier is a noun phrase which indicates some type of measure, as in (97).

(97) in   mouga   kintari
     corn   two   sack
     two sacks of corn

Nouns indicating measure are generally borrowed from Spanish, as indicated in (98).

(98) Ika   Spanish   English
     kintari   quintal   sack
     paketi   paquete   package
     metru   metro   meter
     ribra   libra   pound
     karga   carga   load

Two Ika words used in quantifier phrases are *adžu* 'whole', as in *mʌkki inʔgui adžu* (clothes one whole) 'a whole (change of) clothes', and *džuna* 'kind', as in *mouga džuna inguʌni* (two kind path) 'two kinds of paths'.

3.2. Numerals. Ika numerals are based upon a decimal system. The numerals 'one' to 'nine' are listed in (99).

(99) inʔgui   'one'
     mouga   'two'
     máikʌni   'three'
     maʔkeiwa   'four'
     asewa   'five'
     tšinwa   'six'
     koga   'seven'
     abewa   'eight'
     ikawa   'nine'

Beyond nine, numerals are made up of a phrase naming a number of tens, *uga*, followed by a phrase naming a number of ones, *kʌttou*.

(100) inʔgui   uga   mouga   kʌttou
      one   tens   two   ones
      twelve

For numbers between ten and twenty, *inʔgui uga* is optional.

(101) maʔkeiwa kʌttou
       four   ones
       fourteen

By borrowing Spanish numerals (*sientu* 'hundred', *mir* 'thousand'), it is possible to compose numbers above ninety-nine, as in *sientu mouga uga* (hundred two tens) 'one hundred twenty'.

Juxtaposing two successive numbers indicates an imprecise amount within the range of the two numbers.

(102) mouga máikʌnɨ kʌggi
       two   three   year
       two or three years

Numerals may either precede or follow a noun head, depending on whether the reference is definite or indefinite.[19] Numerals appear before the noun in indefinite reference and after the noun in definite reference. For example, (103) is an indefinite reference to 'man', when a participant is first introduced into a story. In (104), however, the reference to 'one dog' is definite where the previous sentence stated that 'the dog did not come back' and (104) recapitulates that clause.

(103) inʔgui tšeirua -seʔ -ri   wakuma -ri   guako-u-na
       one   man   ERG   TOP   skunk   TOP   kill-AUX-DIST
       A man killed a skunk.

(104) perɨ inʔgui eigui nak-uʔ-nʌ́n   u-ž   -eʔ   nʌngua -ri
       dog   one   also   come-NEG-AUX   AUX-MED   then   and   TOP
       The one dog did not come back, and then ...

Again, (105) and (106) contrast an indefinite and definite reference, respectively, involving the number 'two'. (105) occurs at the beginning of a story, in which the reference to 'two men' is indefinite, while (106) occurs at the end of a story, summing up events involving known participants.

---

[19]Adolfo Constenla suggested to me that definiteness correlates with the order of number and noun, parallel to a distinction in definiteness based on adjective/noun order in Chibchan languages of Costa Rica.

(105) *mouga tšeirua -ri   meina ri-zori -eʔ -ri*
      two   man   TOP   stream 3pS-go then TOP
      Two men went along the stream,...

(106) *tigri   peri mouga nʌ-kʌ-gga   au-ʔ   no*
      jaguar dog   two   1O-PERI-eat AUX-NEG Q
      The jaguar ate my two dogs, didn't it?

A numeral may head a noun phrase, referring to a specific number of items of a previously specified group.

(107) *iwa   mouga -ri   awaʔrei   zoža-na*
      now   two   TOP   below   go-DIST
      Two (men) went below.

3.3. Adjectives. Adjectives and adjective phrases follow the head noun in a noun phrase, as in, *dže kʌntaʔ* (water warm) 'warm water', *unti ziri* (hair fluffy) 'fluffy hair (of a dog)', and *kakarón aroma* (shotgun^shell empty) 'empty shotgun shell'. Rather than occurring alone as in these cases, however, most adjectives occur with *kawa* 'seem' in an adjective phrase.

(108) *tutu   tui   kawa*
      wool^bag   black seem
      black wool bag

(109) *dže   ki   kawa*
      water cold   seem
      cold water

(110) *paka   awʌnʔ   kawa*
      cow   big   seem
      big cow

Repetition of an adjective indicates a greater degree of the quality.

(111) *tšukkui   tšʌmmi   tšʌmmi   kawa*
      rat   yellow   yellow   seem
      a very yellow rat

(112) unti ziri ziri
 hair fluffy fluffy
 very fluffy hair

By postposing -*sin* 'with' to the second of two adjective phrases, it is possible to modify one noun with two adjectives.

(113) tutu   bunsi kawa tui   kawa -sin
 woolˆbag white seem black seem with
 black and white wool bag

3.4. Articles. Although there is no article per se, the demonstrative pronoun *eima* 'this one' occasionally serves to indicate definiteness, while the numeral *in?gui* 'one' may indicate indefiniteness.

(114) eima kusári -ri   an-a-g-u?-nán   u-na
 this deer   TOP   REF-12pS-eat-NEG-AUX   AUX-DIST
 We did not eat the deer.

(115) in?gui tšeirua -se? -ri wakuma -ri   guako-u-na
 one   man   ERG   TOP skunk   -TOP   kill-AUX-DIST
 A man killed a skunk.

3.5. Case marking. Case markers are enclitic in form, occurring as the right-most element of the noun phrase. In (116), -*sin* 'with' is the final element of a noun phrase made up of a possessor phrase and head noun. Further detail concerning case markers is presented in §4.

(116) [bunatši   zʌ-   gei]   -sin
 whiteˆman   GEN   fire   with
 with the whiteman's fire

3.6. Nouns as modifiers. A noun may modify another noun attributively, as in *trapitši kʌn* (press wood) 'wooden sugarcane press' (*trapitši* is from Spanish *trapiche*). A more complex example involves a noun phrase modifying a noun, as in (117). In cases such as these, the modifier noun usually follows the head noun, in the same way as an adjective follows the noun it modifies.

(117) *peri džoʔ motšu*
 dog tail broken
 short-tailed dog (*motšu* is an adjective borrowed from Spanish *mocho*)

4
Case and Postpositions

Syntactic categories of case in Ika include ergative, locative, genitive, instrument, accompaniment, means, and limitative. By case I mean the role of a noun phrase within a clause as overtly indicated by a postposition. Most postpositions which mark these relationships are monosyllabic and phonologically bound, occurring as the last word of the phrase to which they belong. A few postpositions are bisyllabic and are independent, stress-bearing words.

More than one postposition may occur on a single noun or nominalized clause. For example, *pari* 'from' usually combines with a time or locative word in an expression meaning 'from that point on'. The locative word may be one formed by a noun-postposition combination, resulting in two postpositions in a row, as in (118). (119) provides a similar case but contains a nominalized clause rather than a noun.[20] Note that in both (118) and (119), the inner postposition serves as a nominalizer, the outer postposition thus attaching to a nominal element rather than to another postpositional phrase.

(118) *[eim -eki]   pari*
      that LOC   from
      from there

---

[20]See §§4.4, 4.5 and 8.2 for more on locative nominalized clauses.

(119) *[[awion waʔnʌ-ž] -eki] -kin*
 airplane fall-MED LOC LIM
 as far as the airport (where the airplanes fall)

The genitive marker *zei* may occur embedded in a noun phrase which is in turn marked for some other case, but the outer case marker does not apply directly to the phrase with the genitive. In (120), the genitive and noun form a possessor phrase which combines with another noun to form the noun phrase, and it is this noun phrase that takes *-sin* 'with'.

(120) *[[bunatši zʌ-] gei] -sin*
 whiteman GEN fire with
 with the whiteman's fire

The following sections explain the functions of postpositions, beginning with the bound, case marking forms and ending with the phonologically independent forms indicating positional relationships. The genitive marker *zei*, which is sometimes bound and sometimes free, stands between the other two main groups.

4.1. *-seʔ* (locative, source, goal, ergative). The postposition *-seʔ* serves a variety of functions, including marking locative, source, goal, or ergative. As a locative marker, *-seʔ* indicates movement toward or away from a location that is close by, movement into an area, or a position at or on a specified item. In the following examples, the word or phrase to which a postposition pertains is bracketed.

(121) *[uráki] -seʔ kʌtšar -i*
 house LOC arrive while
 arriving at the house

(122) *[aʔkʌtti] -seʔ kʌmʌtša-na*
 cave LOC enter-DIST
 It went into a cave.

(123) *anga tui kawa [kaʔ] -seʔ aʔsʌ-ža*
 bee black seem ground LOC live-MED
 Black bees live on the ground.

The use of *-seʔ* to mark source or goal in transactions is obviously related to its use in marking direction of movement. With some transactional verbs, such as *ʌngeik* 'sell' and *aʔbe* 'deliver', the recipient or goal is marked by *-seʔ*, as in (124).

(124) *Abran -di [Juan] -seʔ kafé   aʔbe   u-ž-in*
      Abran TOP Juan   LOC coffee deliver AUX-MED-WIT
      Abran delivered coffee to Juan.

With verbs such as *san* 'buy', the source, rather than the recipient, is marked by *-seʔ*, as in (125).

(125) *Juan -di [Abran] -seʔ kafé   k-i-sana   u-ž-in*
      Juan TOP Abran   LOC coffee PERI-ʔ-buy AUX-MED-WIT
      Juan bought coffee from Abran.

Each verb depicting a transaction determines whether source or goal is marked by *-seʔ*.

Transitive clauses sometimes show the subject noun phrase marked by *-seʔ*, as in (126).

(126) *[tigri] -seʔ an-ga-na*
      jaguar ERG   REF-eat-DIST
      A jaguar ate it.

Tracy and Levinsohn (1977) suggest that this use of *-seʔ* marks a subject noun phrase referring to a nontopical participant. I argue, in §9.3, that ergative marking is controlled by the position of the agent noun phrase in the clause. When the agent NP occurs contiguous to the verb (rather than in its canonical position before the object) it is marked as ergative. With regard to the alignment of ergative with locative, note that in many of the ergative languages of Australia, the ergative and locative markers are either identical or similar in form (Dixon 1976:313, Blake 1977:51).

4.2. -sin (instrument, accompaniment, conjunction). *-sin* 'with' marks instrument noun phrases, indicates accompaniment, and serves to conjoin noun and adjective phrases. (127) illustrates *-sin* marking an instrument noun phrase.

(127) *[kʌnsia] -sin   si   aʔsir -i*
      vine   with   string tie   while
      He tied it with a vine...

(128) illustrates the use of *-sin* to indicate accompaniment.

(128) *José -ri [Pedru] -sin ʌn-zuei-? nar -i -ri*
José TOP Pedro with REF-go-NEG AUX while TOP
José did not go with Pedro, ...

Note that to say that José did not go does not imply that Pedro also did not go, only that they did not go together. Thus the scope of the negative is the subject noun phrase only and does not include the accompaniment phrase.

Conjoined noun phrases are not very frequent but are constructed by attaching *-sin* to the second conjunct, as in (129).

(129) *Pedru -ri [a] -sin -di gunni win-de?s -i*
Pedro TOP he with TOP hand 3pS-agree while
Pedro Arias and he agreed, ...

In a conjoined noun phrase, the noun that does not bear *-sin* 'with' grammatically heads the phrase. This is rarely a matter of concern, but with bitransitive verbs meaning 'put something down', the shape of the unmarked noun in a conjoined noun phrase controls the selection of verb (§5.3). Compare the verbs of (130)–(132).

(130) *rapi gakó-u*
pencil put^down-AUX
Put the pencil down!

(131) *ribru pa ú*
book put^down AUX
Put the book down!

(132) *ribru [rapi] -sin pa ú*
book pencil with put^down AUX
Put the book and pencil down!

Adjective phrases may also be conjoined by *-sin*, but, as with noun phrases, such constructions are not common.

(133) *tutu bunsi kawa [tuí kawa] -sin*
wool^bag white seem black seem with
black and white wool bag

4.3. -*ikin* (limitative). *-ikin* (limitative) indicates the end point of a period of time or space, 'up to this point/time and no further'. *-ikin* typically occurs with locative constructions including clauses with locative marking meaning 'where X happens', as in (134). (135) and (136) further illustrate the use of -ikin.

(134) eim   -eki pari -ri   žóu-kitši zʌn? waʔkʌ-zar -i
that LOC from TOP all-EMPH just see-AUX   while

[awión   waʔnʌ-ž -eki] -kin
airplane fall-MED   LOC   LIM
From there you can see everything, as far as the airport (where the airplanes fall).

(135) [bin   zán] -ikin nʌ-nʌ-ŋ-waʔk-ʌn-no
when COP   LIM   2S-1O-BEN-look-IMPF-Q
How long (until when) will you wait for me?

(136) [biérne] -kin mi-ŋ-waʔk-ʌn   nʌ-ngua ni
Friday   LIM   2O-BEN-look-IMPF 1O-will   CERT
I will wait for you until Friday.

4.4. -eki (locative). The enclitic -eki (locative) is postposed to nouns and clauses to indicate a location, especially one relatively far away. -eki occurs frequently with demonstrative pronouns, such as eima 'that one', to form a location word meaning 'there' or 'in that place'.

(137) [eim]-eki itšun-nik-ž   -eʔ   -ri
that LOC go^up-when-MED then TOP
When it goes up there...

-eki occurs with nouns which name topographic features to form an adverb of location, often a destination for a motion verb.

(138) [kʌnkʌna] -ki keiwi   zoža-na
forest   LOC right^away go-DIST
He went to the forest.

-eki also occurs with words indicating position, as in bʌkʌna-ki (middle^of-LOC) 'far off in the middle of', or awaʔr-eki (below-LOC) 'far off down below'.

When postposed to a verb-final clause without mood marking, -eki nominalizes the clause as naming a location. Such a nominalized clause is usually stative or imperfective rather than referring to a specific, bounded event.

(139) [aʔkʌttɨ awʌnʔ kawa nuk-ž] -ekɨ itšor -eʔ -ri
cave big seem COP-MED LOC go^up then TOP
He went up to where there is a big cave...

(140) [pérɨ -seʔ kʌ-dan-ʌn nuk-ž] -ekɨ mʌtšei kʌtšar -eʔ -ri
dog ERG PERI-bark-IMPF AUX-MED LOC near arrive then TOP
(They) arrived near where the dog had been barking at something...

With certain nouns, the formative -si comes between the stem and -ekɨ; e.g., urakɨ 'house', but urakɨ-si-kɨ (house-∅-LOC); dže 'river', but dže-si-kɨ (river-∅-LOC).[21]

4.5. -abaʔ (location). The postposition -abaʔ has three locative uses: (a) a case marker for temporal locative expressions, (b) a locative marker for demonstrative pronouns, and (c) a clause nominalizer for specifying the location where something happened. The combination of inɨ 'who, what' and -abaʔ produces the interrogative word inɨbaʔ 'when?'. -abaʔ also occurs on words referring to days of the week (borrowed from Spanish), e.g. runi-baʔ (Monday-LOC) 'Monday'.

-abaʔ has many of the same uses as -ekɨ as a locative marker. Both may occur with demonstrative pronouns to form a word meaning 'there'. (141) illustrates -abaʔ with a demonstrative pronoun.

(141) [až] -abaʔ keiwɨ kʌtšar -i
that^one LOC right^away arrive while
(They) arrived there...

-ekɨ and -abaʔ also both nominalize clauses to name a location. With -abaʔ, however, the embedded clause always involves an action, rather than a state, especially an action involving motion.

---

[21]It is tempting to consider -si as a meaningful segment, but there is no context where a contrast between -si and another suffix or the absense of a suffix shows any semantic difference. In examples, I segment -si as part of the locative suffix.

(142) i?mʌn-eigui [tas   -i   zoža-n] -aba? kʌtšar -e?   -ri
      once-also   look^for while   go-DIST LOC   arrive then TOP
      He arrived once again at the place from which he had gone
      looking...

The difference between *-aba?* and *-eki* may hinge on the nature of *-eki* as deictic and distal. That is, *-eki* points to a specific fixed distant place while *-aba?* merely names a place. This can be seen, for example, in the frequent occurrence of *aža* 'that one' with *-aba?*, while *eima* 'that one pointed to' occurs more frequently with *-eki*. As demonstrative pronouns, *aža* and *eima* differ in that *eima* points to an object located near the speech act, while *aža* serves for anaphoric reference.

4.6. -n (means). The enclitic *-n* (means) marks a noun as the means of performing an action.[22] For example, *kʌttʌ-n* (foot-MEANS) 'by foot' describes a way of traveling. *-n* also combines with language names to specify 'in that language', as in (143). Other examples are *ikʌ-n* (Ika^language-MEANS) 'in Ika', and *peibu-n* (Kogi^language-MEANS) 'in Kogi'.

(143) [bunatšʌ]   -n   -di   azi   a-guak-o
      Spanish   MEANS   TOP   how?   12pS-say-Q
      How do you say it in Spanish?

4.7. zei (genitive). The postposition *zei* marks the genitive case. The genitive is used to indicate part-whole, kinship, and ownership relationships. More generally, the genitive is used to indicate that two nouns are inherently or permanently related to one another.

This case marker is phonologically unique, having two forms *zei* and *zʌ-*. When a genitive precedes its head noun and the head noun is one syllable or otherwise shorter than the genitive, *zʌ-* occurs to mark the preceding form as genitive but is phonologically bound to the following head as a proclitic.

(144) [uraki   zʌ-]   kʌtti
      house   GEN   foot
      main post of house

---

[22]I have seen *-n* attached only to single nouns, not to phrases, but because noun morphology is otherwise virtually nonexistent, I have included the form with the postpositions.

When a head noun is longer than a preceding genitive or when the genitive follows the head noun, phonologically independent *zei* occurs to mark the form it follows as genitive.

(145) *[nʌʔʌn zei] aʔmia*
      1   GEN woman
    my wife

(146) *tšinu [inʔgui zei]*
    pig one GEN
    someone's pig

When the genitive is used to express a kinship relationship, the possessed item is a kinship term while another noun, marked by the genitive, indicates to whom the kinship term pertains, as in (145) and (147).

(147) *[Marta zʌ-] tšeitši*
    Marta GEN father
    Marta's father

In the part-whole use of the genitive, the head noun is the part and the genitive-marked noun is the whole.

(148) *[peri zʌ-] džua*
    dog GEN blood
    dog's blood

In phrases expressing ownership, the head noun is the possessed item and the genitive-marked noun is the possessor.

(149) *[nivi zei] tutusoma*
    we GEN hat
    our hats

In examples involving ownership, the possessor phrase is much more likely to follow the possessed item, as in (146).

Some uses of the genitive do not clearly fall under the headings kinship, part-whole, or ownership. For example, in (150), the possessed noun is *pau*—the 'owner'.

(150) *[anáʔnuga zʌ-] pau*
      animal   GEN owner
      animal's owner

In another case, *bunatši zʌ-gei* (white^man GEN-fire) 'whiteman's fire', this type of fire is neither part of nor owned by but simply is the whiteman's. It is in this sense that the genitive marks an inherent or permanent relationship that usually (but not always) involves kinship, part-whole, or ownership.

4.8. *pari* 'from'. The postposition *pari* indicates the beginning of a time period or the location from which an action is directed. The phrase *mougeʔ pari* (day^after^tomorrow from) conveys the idea of 'from the day after tomorrow on', and *birin pari* (long^ago from) refers to a time span that began long ago, extending toward the present.

In the sense 'the location from which an action is directed', *pari* often occurs with locative words. In (151), *pari* marks a place from which one can see.

(151) *[eim -ekɨ] pari -ri žóu-kɨtši zʌnʔ waʔkʌ-zar -i*
      that LOC from TOP all-EMPH just see-AUX while
      From that place, one can see everything...

pari may also occur postposed to a dependent clause as the last word of a verb phrase. One translation of *pari* in this usage might be 'X happened; from that location, Y'. Often there is a shift in perspective immediately after *pari*, and the event marked by *pari* may be viewed as a climax (of episode), as illustrated in (152). (The postposition is in bold and the clause it marks is bracketed.)

(152) *[anneki, zéi-ʔ-kɨtši nán-ʌkua ni ke-i -eʔ]* **pari**
      no   go-NEG-EMPH AUX-OBL CERT PERI-say then from

      -ri José -ri Pedru -sin ʌn-zuei-ʔ nar -i -ri
      TOP José TOP Pedro with REF-go-NEG AUX while TOP
      "No, you must not go!" he told him, so from that time on José did not go with Pedro...

4.9. *zanɨ* 'be from'. *zanɨ* combines with a noun to define a place or time that is characteristic of something. A typical use of *zanɨ* is to define a person's home.

(153) *[bekɨ]   zanɨ   nʌ-nʌn-ku-e*
      where from   2S-COP-MED-Q
      Where is your home?

(154) *[Jordán]   zanɨ   na-ru-in*
      Jordán   from   COP-1S-WIT
      My home is in Jordán.

zanɨ can be used with a time word, as in *birin zanɨ* (long^ago from), referring to something associated with times past, rather than, as would be the case with *pari*, a time period beginning long ago and extending toward the present.

4.10. Other markers of position. A number of other postpositions indicate position. *tekɨ* indicates a location 'on top of' or 'in the top of' with respect to the noun so marked. For example, *aʔnɨ tekɨ* (rock top^of) 'on top of the rock' and *kʌn tekɨ* (tree top^of) 'in the top of the tree'. Two other indicators of position are *ʌndin* 'under' as in *kaʔ ʌndin* (ground under) 'underground', and *aʔtitéi* 'above'.

5
The Verb Phrase

The major topics of concern in discussing the Ika verb phrase include auxiliary verbs, agreement, aspect, mood, and valence change. §5.2 covers agreement as understood in the normal sense of referencing arguments of the verb by means of verb affixes. §5.3 discusses another type of agreement involving a restricted noun class system as reflected in the predicate. Several paragraphs on valence change cover various operations which affect the number of participants referenced in the verb phrase—causatives, benefactives, reciprocals and reflexives, and comparatives and equatives. A final section discusses the functions of the prefix *an-* (point of reference).

The relative order of the major elements in the verb phrase are presented in (155):

(155) verb (negative) (aspect) (modal) (deictic, mood/connectors)

The lexical verb stem itself is the only obligatory element in the verb phrase. Parenthesized elements sometimes have no overt marker in a given case, though this Ø choice may have significance (e.g., Ø temporal aspect implies PERFECTIVE). There are four parenthesized groups. If the negative suffix occurs, it immediately follows the verb. Temporal aspect markers form the second group (§5.4). Modal suffixes form the third group (§§5.5–10). Deictic suffixes and mood indicators or clause connectors form the fourth group (§5.11 and §7).

There are certain restrictions of occurrence among the suffixes in the verb phrase, although the full extent of these restrictions is not known. For example, the modals *-ngua* (future) and *-nguasi* (purpose) must follow a verb marked by *-ʌn* (imperfective) and *-iza* (result) usually does as well.

Agreement affixes have no fixed location in the verb phrase. Subject affixes include prefixes that occur at the beginning of the phrase and one suffix that occurs at the end of the phrase, *-rua* (first person singular subject). Object markers may appear in two places. Ordinarily they appear prefixed to the lexical verb, immediately following the subject prefix (if present), but when the modal *-ngua* (future) occurs, the object marker references the clause subject and precedes *-ngua* medially in the verb phrase. (§5.2 gives examples of all the agreement affixes; §5.9 presents more detail on *-ngua* with object prefixes.)

5.1. Auxiliary verbs. Auxiliary verbs occur in five contexts. Firstly, stressed, uninflected auxiliary verbs occur in imperatives (§§6.4–6). Secondly, auxiliary verbs occur in sentence introducers, supporting deictic aspect and clause connecting suffixes. These suffixes show the relationship between the final clause of the previous sentence and the first clause of the sentence which the introducer initiates (§7.3). Thirdly, auxiliary verbs occur in questions which help keep conversation flowing, as in (156) and (157).

(156) *eiki   nik-uʔ?   nʌn-no   na-ʔzar   -i   eimai*
      still   work-NEG   AUX-Q   1O-think   while   here

   nako-u-w-in
   come-AUX-PROX-WIT
   I have come thinking, "He is still working, isn't he?"

(157) *kua,   eimei   ki   na-u-ku-e*
      oh   this   CNTR   2S-AUX-MED-Q
      Oh, did you (come) like that?

The last two uses of auxiliary verbs involve the structure of the verb phrase itself; this is discussed in the next two sections. Auxiliary verbs occur obligatorily in the verb phrase to support suffixes which may not occur directly following the main verb itself and occur optionally under specific pragmatic conditions to produce a phrase with an uninflected main verb followed by an auxiliary verb.

The obligatory use of auxiliary verbs. The obligatory use of auxiliary verbs in the verb phrase is controlled by the groups of elements discussed at the beginning of this chapter. As mentioned, the lexical verb is the first element in the phrase, optionally followed by suffixes from four groups.

(158) verb (negative) (aspect) (modal) (deictic, mood/connectors)

As a general rule, the four groups are mutually exclusive. Suffixes from more than one group do not appear together on the same verb. Thus, if both a temporal aspect suffix and a modal suffix occur together in a verb phrase, the lexical verb carries the temporal aspect and the auxiliary verb supports the modal suffix. A major function of auxiliary verbs is to support such additional suffixes when more than one group is represented in a given verb phrase.

In (159) the first verb carries the modal suffix *-ikua* (obligation), and the auxiliary verb *nan*, reduced to *n* in this case, carries the clause, connecting suffix *-ame?* 'because'. The suffix *-kuma* (impersonal) does not enter into the concept of mutually-exclusive groups in the verb phrase, but may combine with suffixes from any group (§9.2).

(159) MODAL   AUX-CONNECTOR
       mi-u-kum-ʌkkua   *n*   *-ame?*
       2O-do-IMPER-OBL   AUX   CAUS
       it had to be done to you because ...

(160) shows a verb phrase in which the lexical verb carries the temporal aspect suffix *-akí* (perfect) while the auxiliary verb carries the deictic suffix marker *-na* (distal).

(160) ASPECT   AUX-DEICTIC
       guak-akí   *nu?-na*
       kill-PRF   AUX-DIST
       It had killed it.

The negative suffix *-u?* requires that the following auxiliary verb (if needed) be *nan*. In (161) the lexical verb carries the negative suffix, the first auxiliary verb carries *-ʌn* (imperfective), and modal *-ngua* (future) serves as its own auxiliary (§5.9).

(161) NEGATIVE   AUX-ASPECT   AUX-MODAL
      nik-uʔ   nan-ʌn   nʌ-ngua
      work-NEG   AUX-IMPF   1O-FUT
      I will not work.

Other suffixes besides the negative also place restrictions on the choice of the following auxiliary verb. *-akí* (perfect) and *-ʌn* (imperfective) (when it is not followed by (future)) require that the following auxiliary be *nuk*. Most of the modal verbs require *nan* as the next auxiliary verb, although *-ikuei* (ability) appears to select either *nan* or *zan*.

The optional use of auxiliary verbs. The auxiliary verb *u* may optionally occur in the verb phrase to produce a phrase with an uninflected verb stem.[23] The optional auxiliary verb follows immediately after the uninflected verb. The lexical verb is usually the uninflected verb in such phrases. Native speakers do not indicate that there is any difference in meaning between verb phrases with and without optional auxiliary verbs, but it appears that the function of optional auxiliaries is to give pragmatic emphasis to the main, lexical verb (§9.9). Most of the examples below contrast two clauses, the first one without an optional auxiliary verb and the second with one. The abbreviation AUX appears above the optional auxiliary.

In both (162) and (163), the only suffix is *-na* (distal deictic aspect), but in (162), the main verb carries this suffix, while in (163) the main verb is uninflected and the following optional auxiliary carries the suffix.

(162)   LEXICAL-DEICTIC
      mouga -ri   awaʔrei   zoža-na.
      two   TOP   below   go-DIST
      Two men went below.

(163) LEXICAL   AUX-DEICTIC
      zoža   u-na.
      go   AUX-DIST
      They went.

In (164) the main verb carries the modal suffix; in (165), it is carried by an auxiliary verb.

---

[23]Uninflected, here, means having no suffixes. Prefixes play a relatively minor role in the verb complex as a whole and apparently have no bearing on the occurrence of optional auxiliary verbs.

(164)
                                    LEXICAL-MODAL
    kʌ́nkʌnʌn   nai-n   zei-kua   ni.
    forest   walk-IMPF   go-OBL   CERT
    Let's go hunting (walk in the forest).

(165)
                                    LEXICAL   AUX-MODAL
    Kʌ́nkʌnʌn   nai-n   zoža   au-kua   nin.
    forest   walk-IMPF   go   AUX-OBL   CERT
    Let's go hunting.

When the negative suffix occurs, it appears in the verb phrase on the main verb, requiring *nan* as a following auxiliary verb. In such cases, an additional auxiliary verb *u* may optionally follow, in which case *nan* is uninflected and is postposed to the main verb as an enclitic.

(166)   LEXICAL-NEG   AUX-DEICTIC
        nʌ-zei-ʔ   *nʌn-na.*
        2S-go-NEG   AUX-DIST
        You did not go.

(167)   LEXICAL-NEG-AUX   AUX-DEICTIC
        kaʔtšon-uʔ-nʌ́n   *u-na.*
        find-NEG-AUX   AUX-DIST
        He did not find it.

Optional auxiliaries may also occur in verb phrases which already contain an obligatory auxiliary verb, as described in the previous section. Both (168) and (169) have a modal suffix followed by an obligatory auxiliary verb carrying the remaining suffixes of a verb phrase. In (169), an optional auxiliary also occurs in the phrase, leaving the main verb without suffixes.

(168)
                 LEXICAL-MODAL   AUX-CONNECTOR
    eimei   mi-u-kum-ʌkkua   n   -ameʔ,
    this   2O-do-IMPER-OBL   AUX   CAUS
    It had to be done to you like this because ...

(169)   LEXICAL   AUX-MODAL   AUX-CONNECTOR
        nʌ-zoža   aw-iza   na   -ndi,
        2S-go   AUX-RES   AUX   COND
        If you were to go ...

The feature common to all Ika verb phrases with optional auxiliary verbs is that the lexical verb is separated towards the left, optionally taking only the negative suffix, with the remainder of the grammatical material occurring to the right, postposed to auxiliary verbs. This grammatical organization serves to highlight the main verb, so that optional auxiliary verbs are especially common in cases where the verb itself constitutes the new information in the clause.[24] Chapter 9 on pragmatics contains a fuller discussion of my conception of the pragmatic structuring of Ika clauses. Suffice it to say, here, that when the comment portion of a topic-comment pragmatic structure consists of only the verb phrase, that phrase is more likely to contain an optional auxiliary verb, giving added prominence or emphasis to the lexical verb itself.[25]

5.2. Agreement. Agreement is shown in Ika by subject and object affixes. Third-person-plural subject is optionally marked, and third-person-singular subject and object are always unmarked, but otherwise, person-marking is obligatory. Subject affixes consistently reference the subject of a clause, but object prefixes serve a variety of functions. The primary function of object prefixes is to mark the grammatical object. When the source or goal of bitransitive verbs is human, the object prefix refers to that participant rather than to the (less animate) object. In conjunction with *kʌ-* (peripheral participant), the object prefixes may reference the possessor of one of the arguments of the verb (§5.13). Finally, object prefixes are involved in the formation of benefactive markers (§5.14).

The subject person affixes are listed in (170). First-person singular is usually unmarked, but *-rua* (first-person-singular subject) occurs in the past and with irrealis forms (as with negatives such as 'I did not go') and statives.[26] Third-person singular is always unmarked. First- and second

---

[24]Hugh Tracy suggested that auxiliary verbs focus on the preceding verb (personal communication), drawing my attention to the possibility that optional auxiliaries have a pragmatic rather than a grammatical function.

[25]These observations concerning frequency of optional auxiliaries are only informal at this point.

[26]The suffix *-rua* (first singular subject) may occur following *-na* (distal deictic aspect) (used in past time references) or following the auxiliary/copular verb *nan*, which usually appears in irrealis contexts, that is, with negatives and modal suffixes. The section on deictic aspect discusses the relationship between aspect and person, and one auxiliary verb appears to have first person bound up with the verb stem itself (*ninza* (first^result)), but apart from these circumstances and *-rua*, there is no overt marking of first person.

Ika

person-plural are both indicated by *a-* (first- or second-person plural subject) but, in practice, are distinguishable by mood. First person is usually declarative and second person interrogative. There is no person marking with imperatives. Special contexts are required for the opposite to occur (e.g., first-person-plural interrogative). *ri-* and *win-* are intransitive and transitive prefixes, respectively, for third plural.[27]

(170)   *-rua ~ ∅*   (first singular subject)
      nʌ-   (second singular subject)
      ∅   (third singular subject)
      a-   (first or second plural subject)
      ri- ~ win- (third plural subject)

A simple paradigm of the verb *tšua* 'see' is presented below to illustrate subject-person marking. Second-person forms are interrogative, as noted above.

(171) *tšua-na-rua*
see-DIST-1S
I saw it.

(172) *nʌ-tšua   u-ž-e*
2S-see   AUX-MED-Q
Did you see it?

(173) *tšua-na*
see-DIST
He saw it.

(174) *a-tšua-na*
12pS-see-DIST
We saw it.

(175) *a-tšua   u-ž-e*
12pS-see   AUX-MED-Q
Did you all see it?

---

[27]Although *win-* usually marks third plural subject with transitive verbs, it also occurs with vowel-initial intransitive verb stems, rather than *ri-*. Landaburu 1985 gives *win-* as potentially referring to second person, a combination which I have not yet observed.

(176) win-tšua-na
　　　3pS-see-DIST
　　　They saw it.

One other suffix, -kuʌr, appears to be a first-person-plural-exclusive form. For example, (177) can describe how many siblings there are in my family.

(177) tšinwa　　nʌ́n-kuʌra　　ni
　　　six　　　　COP-1px　　　CERT
　　　There are six of us.

The context in which this form was elicited made clear that the hearer was not included. (178) also excludes the hearer.

(178) Pablo　-sin　　gou-kuʌra　　ni
　　　Pablo　with　　make-1px　　CERT
　　　Pablo and I (we) made it.

The deictic suffixes (§5.11) also indicate subject person to some degree, although less clearly than the affixes discussed here.

Object person prefixes are presented in (179). As with subjects, third-person-singular object is unmarked. Object prefixes are also used as possessor prefixes on kinship terms. With kinship terms, however, third person is indicated by *a-*, as in *a-tegue* (third-uncle) 'his uncle'.

(179) nʌ-　　　　(first singular object)
　　　mi-　　　　(second singular object)
　　　ø　　　　　(third singular object)
　　　niwi-　　　(first plural object)
　　　miwi-　　　(second plural object)
　　　winʌ　　　(third plural object)

When subject and object prefixes occur on the same verb, the subject prefix precedes the object prefix. In (180), the second-person subject prefix *nʌ-* precedes the first-person-plural object prefix *niwi-* (the final *i* of *niwi-* is morphophonemically lowered to *e* before glottal stop).

(180) nʌ-niwe-ʔzasana　　ki　　　u-ž-e
　　　2S-1pO-pay　　　　　CNTR　AUX-MED-Q
　　　Did you pay us?

The combination of second-person subject and first-person object (both singular) results in the repetition of the form nʌ-.

(181) bin   zan   -ɨkin nʌ-nʌ-ŋ-waʔk-ʌn-no
      when   COP   LIM   2S-1O-BEN-see-IMPF-Q
      How long will you wait for me?

5.3. Locationals and noun classes. A minimal system of noun classes is defined by the physical shape of the objects certain nouns name and the choice of certain verbs or predicate nominals which may occur with those nouns—verbs or nominals which predicate existence, locations, or the notion 'put'. The main classes name long objects (one dimensional), flat objects (two dimensional), three dimensional objects, liquids, containers, or objects with specialized holders. The grammatical correlates of these classes are different words chosen according to the category of the noun, such as *gaka* 'put down long objects', or *pan* 'put down flat objects'.

The noun class system in Ika is minimal in that it involves only nouns referring to concrete objects and the noun classes are only relevant in locational sentences. This type of noun class system is similar to that of the Athapaskan languages (Dixon 1982:223).

Existentials and locatives. Existential and locative clauses make use of noun class indicator plus copula to indicate existence or location. In (182) *aʔkuaskuasɨ* is the noun class indicator for liquids.

(182) tšoʔkuɨ   -seʔ dže   aʔkuaskuasɨ zɨna
      gourd^bowl   LOC   water liquid   COP
      The water is in the bowl. or There is water in the bowl.

The class indicator for three-dimensional objects is *sa*.

(183) akunsi   sʌmmɨ ʌn-sá   zar -i   -ri
      cooked^food   lots   REF-3D   COP while   TOP
      There was a lot of cooked food,...

The same noun may occur with more than one class indicator. For example, in one hunting story, *džua* 'blood' occurs in one case with *aʔkuaskuasɨ* to mean 'a pool of blood' and with *pa* 'flat things' to mean 'spread out or spilled on the ground'.

(184) *džua   ingɨ -ri   a?nɨ tekɨ   a?kuaskuasɨ   zar   -i*
      blood   little TOP   rock top^of liquid   COP   while
      There was a pool of blood on top of a rock...

(185) *perɨ zʌ-džua   papá zɨn -ekɨ*
      dog   GEN-blood   flat COP LOC
      where dog blood was on the ground

The distinction between existential and locative clauses is not always clear. When a referent is known, definite, or topical, it is not generally overtly mentioned, and the clause is taken as locative in nature. When the item is indefinite, new, or nontopical, it will more likely occur as a noun phrase and the clause is interpreted as existential. For example, in (184), the *džua* 'blood' is a new item and the clause is existential; in (186) the item (a deer) is known and not overtly mentioned, and the clause is locational/positional.

(186) *eiki   pá   nar   -e?*
      still   flat   COP   then
      (The deer) was still lying down...

Occasionally, class indicator words help categorize unfamiliar objects by referring to their general characteristics and position. In (187), hunters see something but cannot identify it.

(187) *inɨ   pá   na*
      what   flat   COP
      What is that lying down?

In (188), an unfamiliar item (a sword) is described as both 'like a machete' and *gaka* 'a long thing'.

(188) *Husband: oha   gaka masite   nar   -i   kawa*
                 sword   long machete   COP   while   seem
                 A sword is like a machete.

      Wife: aža   gaka
              that   long
              It's a long thing?

Ika

> Husband: aža gaka hóru -se? aʔžu nus -i
> that long sheath LOC long^be^in COP while
> It's a long thing. It was in a sheath.

Noun classes and verbs meaning 'place'. Verbs meaning 'place something' are sensitive to the nature of the object handled. Example (189) contrasts the verbs for 'put down', which vary according to the class of the object.

(189) kʌn gakó u
stick long^put AUX
Put down the stick!

(190) ribru pa ú
book flat^put AUX
Put down the book!

(191) aʔni sa ú
rock 3D^put AUX
Put down the rock!

(192) pratu tšoʔ ú
plate upright^put AUX
Put down the plate!

Other verbs of placing appear to be derived from the basic verbs for 'put down'. Thus, 'put down flat things' is *pan*, 'put flat things up on' is *ipan*, and 'put flat things into' is *kʌpas*. All the information gathered to date concerning noun class indicators and verbs of placing, location, and existence is presented in (193).

(193) Locational words and noun classes

	Long	Flat	3D	Liquid	Holders	Upright
exist/loc	gaka	pa	sa	——	——	tšo
be in	aʔgeikua	aʔpʌnkua	aʔnikua	aʔkua	aʔžu	aʔnuk
be up on	igeikua	ipʌnkua	inikua	——	ižu	inuk
be on	geikua	pʌnkua	nikua	——	——	nuk
put up on	igeika	ipan	isa	idos	——	itšo
put down	gaka	pan	sa	dos	——	tšoʔs
put in	kʌgaka	kʌpas	kʌssa	kʌdos	kʌžus	kʌtšoʔs

The noun class 'things with holders' refers to such relationships as a machete in its sheath, batteries in a flashlight, legs in pants, or feet in shoes. The key idea is that the holder is designed to contain the item in question. For the verb meaning 'put', only 'put in' is relevant for this class. The noun class 'upright' refers to the position or existence of items such as pots, plates, people, or plants that have a vertical orientation. Note that people and plants only fall into this class when in an upright position. Thus, when approaching a person who is standing, a polite comment is *ei tšo* (thus upright) 'you're standing'. A person is classified as three dimensional (*sa*), however, when sitting. For locative constructions, *a?nuk* (upright^be^in) refers only to plants (i.e., 'be on the ground') while *nuk* (upright^be^on) refers only to people.

Reduplication indicates plurality of an object. Thus, when referring to a book on a table, the proper locational word is *ipa* but for a number of books is *ipapá*.

5.4. Temporal aspect. To understand the marking of temporal relations, it is useful to distinguish the time of an event, some reference point from which that event is viewed, and the time of speaking (Reichenbach 1947). The three choices for temporal aspect— *-akí* (perfect), *-ʌn* (imperfective), and ∅ (perfective)—involve the relationship between the event and the reference point for viewing the event. PERFECT sees an event from its termination, as already completed at (the time of) the reference point, i.e., it indicates that the event referred to is anterior to the reference point. The first clause in (194) sets the reference point for *-akí* as 'by the time the hunters arrive'. With respect to that time, the dogs have already killed the puma cub.

(194) eikɨ   i-ri-tšor   -e?   -ri,   guiadžina   zʌ-   gʌmmɨ
      there   ?-3pS-go^up then TOP   puma   GEN   child

      perɨ   -se?   anʌ-kuss   -i   guak-akí   nu?-na
      dog   ERG   REF-bite   while   kill-PERF   AUX-DIST

They went up there, and the dogs had killed the puma cub, biting it.

IMPERFECTIVE indicates an event going on at the time of the reference point, focussing on the event-in-progress rather than its beginning or end; it covers the same ground as what is usually called progressive in English. In (195), the reference point is the time of speaking. In (196), the reference point is prior to the time of speaking.

(195) inɨ   -ri   ei   kʌ-ž-ʌn-no
what TOP thus PERI-say-IMPF-Q
What are (the dogs) barking at?

(196) emi pari guiadžina zag-ʌn   nuʔ-na
here from puma   steal-IMPF AUX-DIST
A puma was stealing from here.

IMPERFECTIVE may combine with the two suffixes -pan (inceptive) and -bina (motion). INCEPTIVE refers to an event which is beginning to take place or about to take place at the reference point.

(197) ingɨ -ri tšoutšo kʌnak-ʌm-pana keiwɨ
little TOP afraid become-IMPF-INCEP right^away

u-ž   -eʔ   pari -ri, wɨ ʌn-zoža-na
AUX-MED then from TOP ? REF-go-DIST
He began to get scared, and at that point he went.

(198) akín   ora nʌ-k-itšon-ím-pan-ni
as^far^as hour 1O-PERI-go^up-IMPF-INCEP-CERT
It is just about time for me.

MOTION indicates that the subject leaves his primary location to perform the action, then returns to that location once again. For example, (199) does not contain any verb of motion, yet implies that Abram came to eat, then returned to where he had been before.

(199) Abran zamɨ g-ʌm-bina   u-ž-e
Abram food eat-IMPF-MOTION AUX-MED-Q
Did Abram come to eat?

Motion, therefore, marks an action performed while temporarily away from the subject's primary physical point of reference. The motion involved may be either away from or toward the reference point of speaking. That is, the free translation of (199) could be 'Did Abram *go* to eat?' if Abram had been 'at the place of the speech act' and would presumably return.

Not choosing PERFECT or IMPERFECTIVE implies a PERFECTIVE view of an event. That is, the event is seen as an undifferentiated whole. In (200) 'when Pablo came' establishes the point of reference, and (201)–(203) show the three options: (200) César had already gone; (201) he was going;

and (203) simply, he left. *zoža* 'go' is an irregular verb; its varying forms do not represent any differences in meaning.

(200) *Pablo nas -e? -ri*
Pablo come then TOP
When Pablo came,

(201) *César zož-akí nus-in*
César go-PRF AUX-WIT
Cesar had already gone.

(202) *César zuei-n nus-in*
César go-IMPF AUX-WIT
Cesar was going.

(203) *César zor-in*
César go-WIT
Cesar went.

This distinction can also be described as relative tense, in which the reference point is "some point in time given by the context not neccessarily the present moment" (Comrie 1985:56). Comrie defines three relative tenses—simultaneous with, falling before, or falling after the reference point. Looking at (200–203) again, one can see that *-akí* marks an action falling before, *-ʌn* simultaneous with, and *∅* falling after the reference point.

5.5–5.10 Modal Suffixes

There are two sets of elements in the verb phrase which may be said to mark mood—a set of modal suffixes, which are described immediately below, and a set of suffixes and particles which indicate how a dependent clause is connected with its main clause or how an independent clause is related to the speech context. Details related to how two clauses may be related to each other temporally or logically are discussed in chapter 7. The relationships of independent clauses to speech act contexts are discussed in chapter 6.

In the sections which follow here, the seven modal suffixes of Ika—which indicate such concepts as obligation, intention, and ability—are presented. The seven affixes are listed in (204). Since they designate other than actual events, their semantic force is irrealis.

(204) Modal suffixes

>   -ikua   (obligation)
>   -ikuei   (ability)
>   -wiʔna   (prohibition)
>   -iwa   (intention)
>   -ngua   (future)
>   -nguasi   (purpose)
>   -iza   (result)

5.5. -ikua (obligation). -ikua conveys the idea of obligation. A typical use is to give a command without using a grammatically imperative form, as in (205); to indicate hortatory mood, as in (206); or with first person, as in (207).

(205) zéi-ʔ-kɨtšɨ   nán-ʌkua   ni
      go-NEG-EMPH   AUX-OBL   CERT
      You must not go!

(206) nái-n-kɨtšɨ   zʌnʔ kʌnkʌnʌn   núk-ikua   nin
      walk-IMPF-EMPH   just forest   AUX-OBL   CERT
      Let's go hunting (walk in the forest).

(207) bekɨ   ás-ik-o
      where   sit-OBL-Q
      Where should I sit?

5.6. -ikuei (ability). -ikuei (ability) deals with the realm of possibility, —what could take place.

(208) gumiaʔsa   aw   -eʔ   -ri,   ingumʌ́n   tós-ikuei   neika   nin
      cover   AUX   then   TOP   more   catch-ABLE   FOC   CERT

      otiki   -ri
      animal   TOP
      You cover over (the hole) and then you can catch the otiki animal.

(209) kʌ-waʔs   -i   aʔtšón-ʌkuei   zɨn-n   -ekɨ
      PERI-see while   arrive-ABLE   AUX-DIST   LOC
      where you could arrive and see out

(210) *warekɨ zár -i   -gui, kʌ-waʔn au-kuei*
      high   COP while also PERI-fall AUX-ABLE
      Up high like that, they could fall down.

5.7. -wiʔna (prohibition). *-wiʔna* (prohibition) marks an action as something one must never do, for example, drinking kerosene.

(211) *petroriu   aʔga-wiʔna   ni*
      kerosene drink-PROH CERT
      One must not drink kerosene.

The combination of the negative plus *-ɨkua* (obligation), by contrast, only implies that one must not do the action in a particular instance. (212) is from a story in which a hunter has bad luck because he went hunting during Easter week. The verb *naža* 'walk' is a shortened form of the idiom for hunting ('walk in the forest'), and *džuiaʔ* 'day' refers in this case to Easter. Note that one must hunt (*-ɨkua* (obligation)), but one must never hunt during religious holidays (*-wiʔna* (prohibition)).

(212) *nai-kua   neki nai-wiʔna džuiaʔ -seʔ*
      walk-OBL CNTR walk-PROH day   LOC
      One has to hunt, but one should never hunt on that day.

5.8. -iwa (intention). *-iwa* (intention) is a sort of immediate future, expressing intention to do something soon.[28] When a person begins to tell a story s/he may say *kuentu i-wa ni* (story say-INT CERT) 'I'm going to tell a story'. The use of *-iwa* in this formulaic opening to a narrative illustrates the immediacy of the time involved. The reference point for *-iwa* need not be the time of speaking. In (213), the first clause sets the reference point; the use of *-iwa* implies that the second action immediately follows.

(213) *Pablo naʔ-nik-ž   -eʔ -ri, iʔba   zor-iwa   ni*
      Pablo come-when-MED then TOP together go-INT CERT
      When Pablo comes, we will (immediately) go together.

---

[28]The glosses of *-iwa* (intention) and *-pan* (inceptive) give the impression that the two overlap in meaning or function. *-iwa*, however, mainly involves intentionality while *-pan* focusses on the temporal relationship between an event and the point of reference for describing the event, that the event was, is, or will be beginning (or about to begin) at the time of the point of reference.

Ika

5.9. *-ngua* (future) and *-nguasi* (purpose). *-ngua* (future) serves as a general future tense. This modal expresses intention but no particular time frame. In (214), good hunting dogs are characterized as thinking "I will chase all kinds of animals."

(214) pinna džuna was-ʌn   nʌ-ngua
      all   kind   chase-IMPF   1O-FUT
      I will chase all kinds.

Many examples involving *-ngua* imply a general rather than specific intention, as in (214). This modal may also be used, however, with a specific intention. In one hunting story, for example, as a man prepares to fire at his quarry, he thinks 'this shotgun shell is supposed to be able to kill big game' and therefore *guak-ʌn-gua* (kill-imperfective-will) 'it will kill it', referring to this specific case.

-ngua (future) is the only modal which is always marked for person. Person marking with *-ngua* makes use of object-person prefixes. In this sense, *-ngua* parallels the impersonal verbs (§2.6). Combinations of object-person prefixes and *-ngua* are listed in (215).

(215) Person marking for *-ngua* (future)

	singular	plural
1	nʌ -ngua	niwi -ngua
2	mi -ngua	miwi -ngua
3	Ø -ngua	wi -ngua

The modal *-nguasi* (purpose) may be simply a variant of *-ngua* (future). A clause with a verb marked by *-nguasi* is the purpose for the action stated in a second clause. This second clause is indicated in the free translation of (216) but is not included in the vernacular to avoid confusion. At the time when the narrator went to look for his mule, going home was still an intention, so the use of *-ngua* (future) is appropriate. The *-si* could mark this verb as the goal of the main verb, but *-nguasi* appears to have become frozen as a single morpheme; 'X-*nguasi* Y' implies 'do Y in order to X'.

(216) urakɨ -sikɨ zei-n   nʌ-nguasi
      house LOC   go-IMPF   1O-PURP
      (I went to look for my mule) in order to go home.

-ngua (future) (along with *-nguasi*) differs from other modals in that it must follow a verb marked by *-ʌn* (imperfective). The imperfective usually indicates on-going action, as in *dan-ʌn nuk-ža* (bark-imperfective AUX-medial) 'it is barking', but in verb phrases of the type 'verb-imperfective verb' the imperfective expresses purpose or futurity. In (217), *tak* 'look for' carries the imperfective suffix and is the purpose for the second verb, *zoža* 'go'. In terms of the chronological sequence, the speaker first 'went' and later 'looked for', so the verb marked by the imperfective is also future with respect to the final, main verb.

(217) mura ʌn-kʌ-tak-ʌn zoža-na-rua
 mule REF-PERI-look^for-IMPF go-DIST-1S
 I went to look for (my) mule.

-ngua behaves similarly; substituting *-ngua* (future) for *zoža* 'go' produces a structurally and semantically similar construction.

(218) mura ʌn-kʌ-tak-ʌn nʌ-ngua
 mule REF-PERI-look^for-IMPF 1O-FUT
 I will look for (my) mule.

The action 'looking for' is still future and is an intention, but *-ngua* itself has no lexical meaning. Note also that *-ngua* carries person marking in the same way as impersonal verbs, using the object prefixes to mark the subject of the clause. It would seem, then, that this modal is a verb which has become bleached of its lexical content and is becoming (or has become) grammaticized as an indication of intention or future time.

5.10. *-iza* (result). *-iza* (result) marks a verb as indicating what would happen under certain conditions. This idea of 'under the right conditions' can be seen in (219), where the first clause establishes a condition. Combined with the negative, *-iza* implies 'does not want to', as in (220). The form *ninza* is a special form for first person with (result).

(219) Bogotá zoža aw-iza na -ndi, Monserate tšua aw-iza
 Bogotá go AUX-RES AUX COND Monserrate see AUX-RES
 If one were to go to Bogotá, one would see Monserate.

(220) wakuma wima neki g-u? nan-ʌn ninza ni
 skunk meat CNTR eat-NEG AUX-IMPF 1RES CERT
 I would not (do not want to) eat skunk meat.

Unlike *-ngua*, there is no consistent person-marking pattern for *-iza*; for second and third person, the person marking appropriate to the lexical verb is used. In (221), *nʌ-* (2 Subject) and *mi-* (2 Object) are selected for the two main verbs, respectively, as in (221).

(221) *nʌ-zoža   aw-iza   na-ndi,   mouga me-ʔzar-iza   ni*
      2s-go   AUX-RES   AUX-COND   two   2O-feel-RES   CERT
      If you were to go, something bad would happen (lit., 'you would feel two').

In (222), there is no overt marking for person, which is the usual pattern for third person.

(222) *asigeʔ   husiri   tšu-ʌn   zor-iza   neki   tšoutšo*
      next^day   shotgun   see-IMPF   go-RES   CNTR   fear

    kʌnas   -eʔ   pari   -ri
    become   then   from   TOP
The next day he would have gone to see the shotgun (booby-trap) but he got scared.

5.11. Deictic suffixes. One set of verb suffixes indicates deixis in the sense that it signals the relationship between a speaker, an action or state predicated, and a frame of reference. The frame of reference for a dependent clause is an independent clause; that of an independent clause is a speech situation. To interpret these suffixes, one must take into account the subject person of the clause, the time frame, and the context of the clause. The deictic suffixes are listed in (223).

(223) Deictic suffixes
    -w   (proximate first person)
    -ku (medial nonthird person)
    -ž~ø (medial nonfirst person)
    -na (distal/past)

All deictic suffixes except *-na* bear some relationship to subject person, but *-na* simply asserts that an event or state is past time and relatively removed from the present. (224) and (225) illustrate this past time usage of *-na* (distal).

(224) *Biteriu eiki kuʌ-ža*
Viterio there live-MED
Viterio lives there.

(224) *Biteriu eiki kua-na*
Viterio there live-DIST
Viterio lived there.

With *-na*, subject person is indicated by *-rua* (first-person subject), *nʌ-* (second-person subject), or ∅ for third person.

(225) *tšua-na-rua*
see-DIST-1S
I saw it.

(226) *nʌ-tšua-na*
2S-see-DIST
You saw it.

(227) *tšua-na*
see-DIST
He saw it.

Apart from *-na*, deictic suffixes have subject person as one dimension of their meaning. The pattern of person reference is illustrated in the auxiliary verbs of (228) which contrast person of subject and past versus immediate past tense. In all the examples, *-in* (witness) contributes the meaning (past tense) and *nʌ-* (second-person subject) helps disambiguate person reference on the main verb, but all other distinctions of subject person and time are marked by the deictic suffixes.[29]

---

[29]As mentioned in §5.2, second-person forms are usually interrogative, first-person forms declarative. In that sense, the second-person declarative forms in this chart are unnatural and, indeed, it was necessary to generate special contexts in order to elicit a form such as 'you saw it'. My first experiments with eliciting paradigms invariably produced such paradigms as the one given in the section on agreement: 'I saw it. Did you see it? He saw it.' It is possible that speakers of other languages do not have the same difficulty that the Bíntukwa have with this matter, but their reactions highlight the unnaturalness of eliciting paradigms. A few semesters of linguistic training seem to result in a permanent immunity to the feeling that manipulating language in the abstract is an odd sort of thing to do.

(228) Immediate Past   Past

1 tšua   u-w-in   tšua   u-ku-in
   see   AUX-PROX-WIT   see   AUX-MED-WIT

2 nʌ-tšua u-ku-in   nʌ-tšua u-ž-in
   2S-see AUX-MED-WIT   2S-see AUX-MED-WIT

3 tšua   ʌw-∅-in   tšua   u-ž-in
   see   AUX-MED-WIT   see   AUX-MED-WIT

The -w/∅ opposition in the immediate past and -ku/-ž in the past signals the distinction between first and third person, while the -w/-ku contrast for first person and ∅/-ž for third person signal the distinction between immediate and nonimmediate events. As illustrated in (229), ∅ can also be used with second person for the nonimmediate time.

(229) íni   -sin   nʌ-nas-∅-e?
      who?   with   2S-come-MED-Q
      With whom did you come?

(230) buru   -sin   na?-ku-in
      burro with   come-MED-WIT
      I came with the donkey.

Without -in (witness), forms with deictic suffixes lack a past time interpretation. The suffixes -w, -ž, etc. are thus not contributing past tense but relative distance from the deictic center.

(231) beki   nʌ-kuʌ-ža   no
      where? 2S-live-MED Q
      Where do you live?

(232) ʌnke? kua-wa   ni
      here   live-PROX   CERT
      I live here.

The relationship of time or immediacy to deixis is perhaps clearer than that of person-marking to deixis, but person is always defined in terms of the speech situation. The speaker is at the deictic center, motivating the contrast between -w (proximal first person) and -ž/∅ (medial nonfirst person). At a second level, both the speaker and hearer are at the deictic center as coparticipants in the speech situation, and this sharing is reflected in the use of *-ku* for both first and second person.[30]

Temporal deixis is more clearly seen in the contrast between *-w* for 'now' and *-ku* for 'then' for first person, between *-ku* and *-ž* for second person, and between *ø* and *-ž* for third person. Neither subject person nor time fully accounts for the distinctions between deictic suffixes, but together they suggest a ranking for suffixes in which *-w* is the closest to the deictic center (speaker, here), *-ku* is next, followed by *ø* and *-ž*, with *-na* being the most removed from the deictic center, always indicating a past event or state which is less relevant to the here and now.

5.12–5.17 Valence change

Causatives, *kʌ-* (peripheral participant), benefactives, and reciprocals/ reflexives all involve a change in the number of participants referenced by a verb.

5.12. Causatives. Ika has two types of causatives, morphological and analytic (Comrie 1981:160–61). There are two ways to form the morphological causative—the addition of *-s* (causative) and the placement of a syllable boundary after a verb-root-final *n*. Compare *kʌmma* 'sleep' and *kʌmma-s* 'cause to sleep' in (233) and (234).

(233) zizi   hamaka   -seʔ   kʌmm-ʌn   nuʔ-na
      baby   hammock   LOC   sleep-IMPF   AUX-DIST
      The baby was sleeping in the hammock.

(234) Marta   zizi   hamaka   -seʔ   kʌmma-s-ʌn   nuʔ-na
      Martha   baby   hammock   LOC   sleep-CAUS-IMPF   AUX-DIST
      Martha rocked the baby to sleep in the hammock.

The pair of verbs *tšon* 'enter' and *tšuŋ* 'let someone enter' illustrate the second strategy. The forced syllable boundary after the *n* of *tšon* manifests

---

[30] Landaburu presents an analysis similar to this which treats these suffixes, with the exception of *-na* (considered to have no relation to the other suffixes), as markers of subject. His analysis hinges around a basic distinction between the participants in the speech situation versus 'the world', further subdividing the participants in the speech situation between the speaker himself and various sets of referents, including both first and second plural.

itself in the raising of *o* to *u* (§1.16) and in the velar articulation of *n* as [ŋ] to form *tšuŋ* (§1.15), as illustrated in (235).

(235) mi-tšuŋa   u-ž-e
       2O-CAUS^enter   AUX-MED-Q
       Did he let you go in?

(236) nʌ-tšuŋa   u-ž-in
       1O-CAUS^enter   AUX-MED-WIT
       He let me go in.

All the noncausative-causative pairs involving -*s*, that I have identified, are listed in (237). Those involving a syllable boundary after *n* are listed in (238). Note that in a few pairs, a verb is derived from an adjective by the causative suffix.

(237)   Regular Form   Causative Form

        aʔkanʌn   'shout'   aʔkʌnsʌn   'play a musical instrument'
        arukʌn   'go up'   arusʌn   'lift'
        duʔnʌn   'be dry'   dussʌn   'make dry'
        gʌrʌnna   'be broken'   garʌssʌn   'break'
        inažʌn   'grow up'   ineisʌn   'rear'
        kʌmmʌn   'sleep'   kʌmmasʌn   'put to sleep'
        mawʌn   'cry'   mousʌn   'make someone cry'
        pátiro   'be smooth'   patirusʌn   'make smooth'
        reʔwʌrisʌn 'undress'   reʔwʌrʌssʌn 'undress someone'
        wasʌn   'fall'   wʌssʌn   'fell a tree'
        žʌn   'be smooth'   žʌnsʌn   'scrape, shave'

(238)   Regular Form   Causative Form

        aʔtšonʌn   'go out'   aʔtšuŋʌn   'take out'
        aʔwanʌn   'vomit'   aʔwʌŋʌn   'make vomit'
        itšonʌn   'go up'   itšuŋʌn   'put up'
        kʌtšanʌn   'go down'   kʌtšʌŋʌn   'get something down'
        tanʌn   'damage'   tʌŋʌn   'damage another's property'
        tšanʌn   'enter'   tšuŋʌn   'let enter'

Analytic causatives involve two verbs, one of which specifically means CAUSE. The verb *guaʔsa* 'make, cause' occurs with an imperfective verb as its complement, to convey the idea 'make someone do X'.

(239) *Juan -se? tšei tšus-ʌn gua?sa-na*
       Juan ERG farm leave-IMPF cause-DIST
       Juan made him leave his farm.

With the negative suffix, *gua?sa* indicates 'cause not to X' or 'prevent from doing X' rather than 'did not cause to X'; the scope of negation is the subordinate verb rather than *gua?sa* itself.

(240) *ši   wis-ʌn   neki   gua?s-u?   nar   -i*
       foul^odor spray-IMPF CNTR   cause-NEG AUX   while
       (She) did not let the (skunk's) scent spray out, or
       (She) kept the (skunk's) scent from spraying out.

The causee is referenced on *gua?sa* by object prefixes. *gua?sa* always involves the idea of force—making the causee do something s/he would not otherwise do.

(241) *zož-ʌn   mi-gua?sa   u-ž-e*
       go-IMPF   2O-cause   AUX-MED-Q
       Did he make you leave?

(242) *nʌ-gua?sa-na*
       1O-cause-DIST
       He made me (leave).

5.13. *kʌ*- (peripheral participant) and valence increase. The prefix *kʌ*- (peripheral participant) increases a verb's valence by allowing it to take an object-person prefix referring to an additional participant. With some verbs, this peripheral participant is implied but may not be overtly expressed in the clause. In other cases, the additional participant may be expressed as the possessor of one of the named participants in the action.

For example, *ža* 'say' semantically implies a hearer but may not grammatically refer to that hearer without adding *kʌ*-. (Compare *ža-na* (say-DISTAL) 'he said' with *nʌ-kʌ-ža-na* (1O-PERIPH-say-DISTAL) 'he said to me'. Similarly, *wa?k* 'look' is grammatically intransitive, although the act of looking implies what is seen. In order to add an object prefix, it is necessary to use *kʌ*-, as in *mi-ka-wa?ka* (2O-PERIPH-look) 'it looks at you'. The verb *tšua* 'see', on the other hand, is transitive and may take an object-marking prefix without *kʌ*-.

The verb *ʌngeik* 'sell' is grammatically transitive, even though it implies a buyer. To explicitly refer to the buyer, either by a separate noun phrase or a first- or second-person object prefix, it is necessary to use *kʌ-*. Compare (243) and (244).

(243) *kafé   ʌngei?-na-rua   ni*
      coffee sell-DIST-1S   CERT
      I sold coffee.

(244) *kafé   Pablo -se? k-ʌngei?-na-rua   ni*
      coffee Pablo LOC   PERI-sell-DIST-1S CERT
      I sold coffee to Pablo.

The introduction of a named possessor of one of the clause participants by use of *kʌ-* is illustrated with the verb meaning 'eat'. With transitive verbs, *kʌ-* indicates the possessor of the object. In (245), the second-person object prefix *mi-* refers to the object of the verb while, in (246), because of the presence of *kʌ-*, it refers to the possessor of the object.

(245) *tigri   mi-ga*
      jaguar   2O-eat
      The jaguar eats you.

(246) *peri -kin -di   mi-kʌ-ga*
      dog   LIM   TOP   2O-PERI-eat
      (The jaguar) eats your two dogs.

Sentence (247) illustrates a first-person possessor of an object with the transitive verb meaning 'weed'.

(247) *betši   nʌ-k-a?gaw-ʌn   nuk-ža   ni*
      maguey   1O-PERI-weed-IMPF   AUX-MED   CERT
      He is weeding my maguey.

With locative/existential clauses, a possessor is associated with the location. Sentence (248) predicates the existence of a shotgun shell and names a shotgun as the place where the shell is located. The combination of first-person object marker and *kʌ-* (peripheral participant) indicates that the speaker is the possessor of the shotgun.

(248) *husiri   kakʌrón   neki   nʌ-k-a?nik-u?   na-?   no*
      shotgun   shell   CNTR   1O-PERI-3D^be^in-NEG AUX-NEG   Q
      There is no shell in my gun, is there?

In (249), a handbag is the specified location, and the peripheral participant is the possessor of the handbag.

(249) tšegekuána -seʔ aʔburu   k-aʔnikua-na
      handbag   LOC offering   PERI-3D^be^in-DIST
      There was an offering in his handbag. *or* He had an offering in his handbag.

With intransitive verbs, *kʌ-* indicates the possessor of the subject.

(250) husiri   neki   k-aʔwi-uʔ   nʌn-na
      shotgun   CNTR   PERI-fire-NEG   AUX-DIST
      His shotgun didn't fire.

This particular usage of *kʌ-* is similar to what Relational grammarians call POSSESSOR ASCENSION (Frantz 1981:28-30; Allen, Gardiner, and Frantz 1984:306-07). As is apparently the case with other instances of possessor ascension, the possessor is here associated with the most oblique noun phrases present—subject of intransitive, object of transitive, source/goal of bitransitive, or location of locative/existential clauses.

5.14. Benefactives. BENEFACTIVE is signalled by *ŋ-* for first and second person and by *i-* for third person, in combination with object person prefixes.[31] Compare (251) with (252), which shows *nʌ-* (1 Object) plus *n-* (BENEFACTIVE).

(251) kafé   zas-ʌn   nuk-ž-in
      coffee save-IMPF   AUX-MED-WIT
      He is saving coffee.

(252) kafé   nʌ-n-zas-ʌn   nuk-ž-in
      coffee 1O-BEN-save-IMPF   AUX-MED-WIT
      He is saving coffee for me.

In (253), *i-* (benefactive) indicates that the action is performed for the benefit of another.

---

[31]Intervocalically, *ŋ-* (benefactive) always has a velar point of articulation. The underlying form of the morpheme, therefore, always has a syllable boundary following it (§1.15).

(253) *Juan urakɨ i-gaw-ʌn nuk-ža ni*
Juan house BEN-make-IMPF AUX-MED CERT
Juan is making a house for someone.

Although third-person-singular object is unmarked, third plural is indicated by *winʌ-* (with ʌ deleted preceding *i*).

(254) *akusa win-i-zas-ʌn nuʔ-ku-in*
needle 3pO-BEN-save-IMPF AUX-MED-WIT
I'm saving needles for them.

The benefactive markers are also used in a malefactive sense.

(255) *Juan nʌ-n-guʔ-na*
Juan 1O-BEN-pick^up-DIST
Juan took it from me (to my detriment).

Some verbs may occur with either the benefactive marker or *kʌ-* (peripheral participant). In such cases, benefactive indicates a more direct involvement in the action than *kʌ-*. Compare *nʌ-ŋ-unaʔ-na* (1O-BEN-bring-DIST) 'he brought me' and *nʌ-k-unaʔ-na* (1O-PERIPH-bring-DIST) 'he brought something to me'. With benefactive, the person referenced by an object prefix is directly affected whereas the referent of *kʌ-* is only a recipient.

Some benefactive forms are idioms. *waʔk* usually means 'look', but means 'wait for' with the benefactive.

(256) *mi-ŋ-waʔk-ʌn nus-e*
2O-BEN-look-IMPF AUX-Q
Was he waiting for you?

With the copula *zan*, the benefactive indicates years of age.

(257) *máikʌnɨ uga kʌggi nʌ-n-zɨ-ni*
three tens year 1O-BEN-COP-CERT
I am thirty years old.

5.15. Reciprocals and reflexives. Reciprocals and reflexives are marked by *riŋa-* (reciprocal).[32] In the absence of overt noun phrases, it is not always clear whether reciprocal or reflexive meaning is intended.

[32] As with *ŋ-* (benefactive), the *n* of *riŋa-* has velar articulation, the underlying form of the morpheme showing a syllable boundary following the *n*.

(258) *riŋa-tšua   u-ku-in*
      RECIP-see   AUX-MED-WIT
      We saw each other *or* I saw myself.

With an overt noun, the postposition *-sin* 'with' indicates reciprocal action.

(259) *Pablo   -sin   riŋa-tšua   u-w-in*
      Pablo   with   RECIP-see   AUX-PROX-WIT
      Pablo and I (just) saw each other.

riŋa- usually occurs with first-person-singular verb forms (§5.11). The adjective *kingui* 'same' following a subject noun indicates a reflexive reading of *riŋa-*.

(260) *a   kingui   riŋa-sua   u-ž-in*
      3   same   RECIP-burn   AUX-MED-WIT
      He burned himself.

kingui is also used in emphatic forms, such as 'he himself did it'.

5.16. Comparatives and equatives. Comparison is indicated by associating the postposition *guasi* with a standard of comparison in conjunction with the adjective *ingumʌ́n* 'more'. In (261), *Juansitu* is the standard of comparison and *ingumʌ́n nʌža* (more walk) means 'walk faster'.

(261) *Pedru   Juansitu   guasi   ingumʌ́n   nʌža   ni*
      Pedro   Juancito   CF   more   walk   CERT
      Pedro walks faster than Juancito.

In the following two examples, *ingumʌ́n*, with benefactive and copula, indicates 'is older'.

(262) *Dawid   nʌʔʌn   guasi   ingumʌ́n   i-zin-ni*
      David   1   CF   more   BEN-COP-CERT
      David is older than me.

(263) *nʌʔʌn   Juan   guasi   ingumʌ́n   nʌ-n-zin-ni*
      1   Juan   CF   more   1O-BEN-COP-CERT
      I am older than Juan.

Equation is indicated by the postposition *-sin* 'with' marking the standard and *dikin* 'same' as the adjective. In (264), *ma* 'you' is the standard for the equation, and the comparison is one of height. (265) illustrates a predicate adjective construction meaning 'be strong'.

(264) *Juan ma -sin dikin kawa no*
    Juan 2 with same seem Q
    Is Juan the same height as you?

(265) *buru mouga nʌʔʌn zei múra -sin dikin džuma aʔnikuʌ-ža*
    burro two 1 GEN mule with same strong 3D^be-MED
    My two burros are as strong as the mule.

Note that the standard of comparison is an oblique constituent, not referenced on the verb. (266) is a single-participant descriptive clause in which *kawa* 'seem' is an impersonal verb, referencing the participant by an object prefix. The addition of a standard of comparison in (267) does not alter person marking, and a reversal of participants in (268) results in a corresponding change of object marker on the verb.

(266) *ma deiru mi-kawa ni*
    2 thin 2O-seem CERT
    You are thin.

(267) *ma nʌʔʌn guasi deiru mi-kawa ni*
    you 1 CF thin 2O-seem CERT
    You are thinner than I.

(268) *nʌʔʌn ma guasi deiru nʌ-kawa ni*
    1 2 CF thin 1O-seem CERT
    I am thinner than you.

5.17. *an-* (reference). The verb prefix *an-* (reference) occurs primarily in two environments—with transitive verbs to indicate a nonhuman object, and with motion verbs to identify a significant place with respect to which the motion takes place. In both uses, the key idea is that of fixing a point of reference towards which action is directed. The prefix has the form *ʌn-* when followed by a consonant-initial form, resulting in a closed syllable.

With transitive verbs, *an-* indicates a nonhuman object, usually one directly affected by an action with a high degree of carry-over from agent to patient. In (269) *an-* occurs on *guak* 'kill' and *ga* 'eat', illustrating the direct impact of the action on the nonhuman object.

(269) dže -sikɨ ʌn-guak-akɨ́ nus -i   -ri, ingɨ -ri
      river LOC REF-kill-PRF AUX while TOP   little TOP

      ʌn-g-ʌn   nus -eʔ keiwɨ   kʌtšʌn-na
      REF-eat-IMPF   AUX   then right^away arrive-DIST
      Having killed (the deer) at the river, (the dogs) were eating on it when he arrived.

an- often occurs with verbs which inherently imply a direct effect on the object—verbs such as *aʔtʌri* 'skin an animal', *aʔsi* 'tie up', and *gos* 'carry'. Other verbs imply less contact, such as *tšua* 'see' and *dan* 'bark'. In all cases, however, *an-* (reference) indicates that an object is the focus of attention.

With motion verbs, *an-* singles out a location as a significant point with respect to which the motion takes place. In this way, *an-* helps distinguish directed and undirected motion. That is, a motion verb without *an-* predicates movement without being specific about the location involved. (270) is a leave-taking which focusses on a departure while (271) focusses on the goal of motion.

(270) zor-iwa   ni
      go-INT   CERT
      I'm going now.

(271) Nabusímake ʌn-zor-iwa ni
      Nabusímake REF-go-INT CERT
      I'm going to Nabusímake.

Within narratives, *an-* helps define physical scenes. For example, hunting stories involve a great deal of movement as hunters leave home to track game, follow particular animals, return home, and later resume the hunt. Only a few instances of motion verbs, however, are marked by *an-*. These cases usually involve motion towards significant locations in a story. When the hunter returns to his home, the verb usually carries *an-*; a person's house as his home base is an inherently important location. As a story progresses, however, narrators use *an-* to define a place around which a segment of the story revolves. In hunting stories, these are places such as where game is sighted or where a chase ends and a kill is made. Movements toward these spots often are marked by *an-* while other verbs of motion are not so marked.

This use of *an-* (reference) to mark a significant location is similar to the use of 'come' and 'bring' in English. Fillmore suggests that these verbs may serve to define points of reference within narratives (1975:67):

> *Come* and *bring* also indicate, in discourse in which neither speaker nor addressee figures as a character, motion toward a place taken as the subject of the narrative, toward the location of the central character at reference time, or toward the place which is the central character's home base at reference time.

naka 'come' is very infrequent in narratives in my data and apparently is defined with reference to the speaker, not to characters within the story. *an-*, however, combines with other motion verbs to serve the same purpose of indicating significant locations within a narrative.

Clauses in which *an-* (reference) figures often show features of high transitivity, as defined by Hopper and Thompson 1980. In a general sense, transitivity is seen as "the effective carrying over of an activity from an A[gent] to a patient" (1980:279), but more specifically, Hopper and Thompson suggest that transitivity be broken down into a number of components defining scales along which a given clause can be ranked as more or less transitive. Those components of interest with regard to *an-* are number of participants, kinesis, volitionality, affectedness of the object, and individuation of the object.

Motion verbs with specific locations have more participants than those with no location or those with a nonspecific location. The verbs on which *an-* appears are usually kinetic, involving action as opposed to states (an exception to this is a verb such as *tšua* 'see'). Clauses with *an-* usually show volitionality of an agent and an affected object, often with a direct impact of the agent on the object (with verbs like 'kill' and 'eat'). Finally, in clauses with *an-*, the object or location is almost always highly individuated; that is, it is referential, concrete, and definite rather than nonreferential, abstract, and indefinite.

6
Clause Formation

This chapter covers the formation of basic clause types, declaratives, questions, and imperatives; it deals as well with negation, a topic whose scope is within the clause.

6.1. Declaratives. Declarative mood is marked by *ni* (certainty), *-in* (witness), or is unmarked. *-in* indicates that the speaker witnessed the event predicated in the immediate or recent past. *ni* (certainty) may be associated with any time frame, but indicates either that the speaker did not witness the event or that the event is removed in time, space, or relevance to the present. Compare the question in (272) with the answers (273), using *-in*, and (274), using *ni*.

(272) *win-naka   u-ž-e*
      3pS-come   AUX-MED-Q
      Did they come?

(273) *win-naka   u-ž-in*
      3pS-come   AUX-MED-WIT
      They came (and I saw it).

(274) *win-naka   u-na   ni*
      3pS-come   AUX-DIST CERT
      They came (but I didn't see it).

-in (witness) indicates greater local immediacy than *ni*. In (275), *ni* refers to 'around here in general'. In (276), *-in* emphasizes 'right here where we are speaking'.

(275) ʌnke? kua-wa ni
      here   live-PROX CERT
      I live here (in this area).

(276) ʌnke? kua-w-in
      here   live-PROX-WIT
      I live right here.

-in (witness) may also indicate temporal immediacy. In (277) and (278), the question and answer refer to an event going on at the time the exchange takes place which the asker cannot see but which the answerer does.

(277) nugue a-o
      stop   AUX-Q
      Are they stopping? *or* Did they stop?

(278) nugue ʌw-in
      stop   AUX-WIT
      They stopped.

ni (certainty) occurs in several contexts in which *-in* (witness) does not occur—in descriptive clauses (with predicate nominals and adjectives), in clauses with modal suffixes, and in statements that are generally true but that do not refer to a specific event. Example (279) illustrates *ni* in a descriptive clause. In (280), *ni* occurs with the modal *-ikua* (obligation). Example (281) shows *ni* in a clause which is generally true rather than referring to a specific case.

(279) tigri   ni
      jaguar   CERT
      It's a jaguar.

(280) kʌ́nkʌnʌn nai-n   zoža au-kua   nin
      forest   walk-IMPF   go   AUX-OBL   CERT
      Let's go hunting.

(281) gagáru   -ri   kʌniu   gʌ-ža   ni
      animal   TOP   cane   eat-MED CERT
      The gagaru animal eats sugar cane.

ni (certainty) is not always present in sentences where it might be expected. Within narrative, especially, mood marking may be absent on final independent clauses. The narrative establishes an environment in which unmarked clauses are understood as declarative. Declarative sentences in isolation also may lack mood marking.

An additional context in which declarative mood markers occur is in indirect content questions. (282) shows *ni* occurring with *ini* 'what?' in an indirect question (§8.5).

(282) ini   ni   neki   aʔza-ʔ   nʌn-na
      what?   CERT   CNTR   think-NEG   AUX-DIST
      He didn't know what it was.

6.2–6.3 Questions

There are three kinds of questions in Ika—yes/no questions, content questions, and indirect questions. All interrogative sentences are marked on the final, independent clause of the sentence by one of the verb-phrase-final suffixes or particles: *-e*, *-o*, or *no*. *-e* (interrogative) covers past time; *-o* and *no* occur in questions referring to the present, the future, or the distant past. Content questions also use special question words which are generally in clause-initial position. Indirect content questions utilize the question words but use declarative mood marking in the verb phrase.

6.2. Yes/No questions. There are three types of yes/no questions —neutral, alternative, and leading questions (expecting a yes or no response). A neutral yes/no question is formed by adding one of the interrogative suffixes or the interrogative adverb *no*, as in (283) and (284).

(283) mari   me-ʔzan-o
      hunger   2O-think-Q
      Are you hungry?

(284) win-naka   u-ž-e
      3pS-come   AUX-MED-Q
      Did they come?

no (interrogative) occurs following forms such as the medial deictic suffix or *-ngua* (future) that do not allow an interrogative suffix and in clauses with predicate nominals (which usually have no copula to refer to the present). These three cases are illustrated in the following three examples, respectively.

(285) *Jordán nʌ-kuʌ-ža no*
 Jordán 2s-live-MED Q
 Do you live in Jordán?

(286) *sige? zei-n mi-ngua no*
 tomorrow go-IMPF 2O-FUT Q
 Will you go tomorrow?

(287) *sisio no*
 bird Q
 Is it a bird?

An alternative yes/no question combines two questions, each beginning with *kua* 'or', as in (288); although examples from conversation suggest that it is possible to give only *kua* plus the second alternative as the second part of the question, as in (289).

(288) *kua kusari ki nan-ʌn no kua guiadžina ki*
 or deer CNTR COP-IMPF Q or puma CNTR

  nan-ʌn no
  COP-IMPF Q
 Is it a deer or is it a puma?

(289) *mʌtšéi ʌn-zagítš-ik-o, kua peiki nar -i*
 near REF-pass-OBL-Q or far COP while
 Do they pass near (each other) or far away?

A leading yes/no question ends in *no* (interrogative) or the phrase *na-? no* (be-negative interrogative).

(290) *peibu -se? -ri diwʌn kaw -i tutusoma isʌ-ža*
Kogi ERG TOP different seem while hat sew-MED

              TAG-NEG
kawa na-?   no
seem COP-NEG Q
It seems that the Kogi people make their hats differently, doesn't it?

Leading questions are an interrogative form often used to express opinions. When the lexical verb and the tag are either both negative or both positive, the question expects a negative reply. When one is negative and the other is positive, the question expects a positive reply. A negative tag always has the form *na-?* (be-negative); a negative in the verb phrase usually appears on the lexical verb but may also appear on an auxiliary verb.

In (290), the verb is positive and the tag is negative, thus expecting a positive reply. In (291), the verb is negative but the tag is positive, also expecting a positive reply. The first free translation follows the Ika negation pattern; the second is more idiomatic English.

(291)   LEXICAL-NEG TAG
eima -ri džuirí a?za-?   no
that TOP soft COP-NEG Q
These are not soft, are they? (literal)
These are soft, aren't they?

Example (292) illustrates a negative verb and a negative tag, expecting a negative reply ('No, my shotgun does not have a shell in it.'). The fourth possibility, a positive verb with a positive tag, expects a negative reply, as in (293).

(292)   LEXICAL-NEG   TAG-NEG
husiri kakʌrón neki nʌ-k-a?nik-u?   na-?   no
shot^gun shell CNTR 1O-PERI-be^in-NEG be-NEG Q
My shotgun doesn't have a shell in it, doesn't it? (literal)
My shotgun doesn't have a shell in it, does it?

(293)   LEXICAL   TAG
makʌri -seʔ aweri eimei kaw -i   ki   g-ʌn   no
vulture ERG ?   like^this seem while CNTR eat-IMPF Q
A vulture eats like this, does it? (literal)
A vulture doesn't eat like this, does it?

This fourth possibility is rare in my data. A positive verb with a positive tag is indistinguishable in form from a yes/no question. In these cases, the context enables a determination of whether the speaker is expressing an opinion or genuinely asking for information. Example (293) comes in a context where the speaker examines a goat which a predator killed. After examining the animal, he states (293), lists the relevant data, then says the following:

(294) *guiadžina -seʔ ga-na   guin kaw -eʔ   -ri*
      puma   ERG eat-DIST ?   seem then   TOP
      It seems that a puma killed it...

In the context, then, it is clear that the speaker is not asking, "Does a vulture eat like this?" but is stating his opinion that "A vulture does not eat like this." At the same time, the potential confusion between a leading question of this form and a neutral yes/no question may motivate speakers to choose, instead, a leading yes/no question with both negative verb and negative tag, to give a negative reading to the whole sentence.

One possible variation in the tag is the addition of *nʌn* 'be', implying that the situation being asked about is removed in space. In (295), *na-ʔ no* (be-negative interrogative) implies locative and temporal immediacy, while in (296) *na-ʔ nʌn-no* (be-negative be-interrogative) implies locative distance.

(295) *reró wiehu kawa na-ʔ   no*
      watch old   seem COP-NEG Q
      The watch seems old, doesn't it? (speaker is looking at the watch)

(296) *reró wiehu kawa na-ʔ   nʌn-no*
      watch old   seem COP-NEG be-Q
      The watch seems old, doesn't it? (the watch is somewhere else)

6.3. Content questions. Content questions utilize clause-final interrogative marking plus special question words that generally occur clause-initially, as in (297).

(297) bekɨ   nʌ-zoža   no
     where? 2s-go   Q
     Where are you going?

Ika question words are listed in (298). The discussion of these question words follows the order of their listing, from those questioning noun phrases, to those questioning elements within noun phrases, to those questioning adverbial constituents such as time and manner.

(298) inɨ (-baʔ) 'who?, what day?'
      bema   'which one?'
      biga   'how many?'
      bindi   'how many?, how much?'
      bekɨ   'where?'
      bin zan   'when?'
      iari   'why?'
      azi   'how?'

inɨ 'who?, what?' is the interrogative word for noun phrases. *inɨ* may reference a subject, object, or oblique NP. In (299) the questioned constituent is the subject.

(299) inɨ   -ri   nai-n   nuk-o
      what?   TOP   walk-IMPF   AUX-Q
      What is walking (by)?

When the object is questioned, the subject, as given information, is usually not overtly mentioned in the clause.

(300) inɨ   was   -i   -ri   ei   ž-ʌn   no
      what? chase while TOP   thus   say-IMPF   Q
      What is it chasing, barking like that?

The occurrence of a question word at the beginning of a clause, as in (300) does not give clear evidence that the question word has been fronted or moved from a position after the subject. Declarative clauses without overt subject noun phrase and with object in sentence-initial position are frequent in text, suggesting that question words in sentence-initial position could be due to a pattern of zero anaphora rather than to movement. In (301), the noun phrase questioned is the object of the postposition *sin* 'with'.

(301) ini   -sin   nʌ-nas-e
    what?   with   2s-come-Q
    With whom did you come?

The question word *iniba?* 'what day?' is derived from *ini* by the addition of *-aba?*, which is also found in words for days of the week borrowed from Spanish. *iniba?* asks for a specific day of the week in reply, as opposed to *bin zan* 'when?', which asks for any sort of time word in reply. In the following exchange, a wife's initial question is not clear to her husband, so he shifts the question from *bin* 'when?' (in general) to *iniba?* 'what day?'.

(302)   Wife: bin   zar   -i   -ri   a-zori-e
                 when?   COP   while   TOP   12pS-go-Q
                 When did you all go?

        Husband: iniba?   zar-e
                 what^day?   COP-Q
                 What day was it?

        Wife: iniba?   nʌ-zoža   nan-ʌn   no
                 what^day?   2s-go   AUX-IMPF   Q
                 On what day did you go?

        Husband: bierne   Monserrate   a-zori-n
                 Friday   Monserrate   12pS-go-WIT
                 We went to Monserrate on Friday.

The question word *bema* 'which one?' also questions a noun phrase but refers to one member of a set of possibilities.

(303)   bema   gowiernu   uraki   no
        which^one?   government   house   Q
        Which one is the government building?

biga 'how many?' is the interrogative word corresponding to numbers. It may combine with *-muru* 'times' to indicate 'how many times'.

(304)   biga   miri   ga-na   no
        how^many?   thousand   eat-DIST   Q
        How many thousand did they eat?

(305) bigá-muru   nʌ-zori-e
      how^many?-times   2s-go-Q
      How many times did you go?

An answer to *bigámuru* would be one of several adverbs utilizing *-muru*, as in *mú?-muru* (two-times) 'twice' or *mái-muru* (three-times) 'thrice'.

The question word *bindi* 'how much?' does not necessarily ask for a number in reply, as *biga* does. (306) might be a follow-up question to a person saying, "I sold some coffee."

(306) bindi   nʌ-ngeis-e
      how^much?   2s-sell-Q
      How much did you sell?

The question word *bekɨ* 'where?' is the interrogative locative word. Note in (307) that the postposition *pari* 'from' immediately follows *bekɨ*; postpositions always immediately follow the question word to which they pertain.

(307) bekɨ   pari nʌ-nas-e
      where?   from 2s-come-Q
      Where did you come from?

The question word *bin zan* is the interrogative form for time expressions; the actual question word *bin* 'when?' apparently always occurs with the copula *zan*.

(308) bin   zan-o
      when?   COP-Q
      What time is it?

(309) bin   zar   -i   -ri   a-zori-e
      when?   COP   while TOP   12pS-go-Q
      When was it that you went?

The question word *iari* 'why?' questions purpose or cause. (310) uses a motion verb with a purpose complement (§8.6) to answer *iari* 'why?'.

(310) iari   zei-n   mi-ngua   no
      why?   go-IMPF   2O-FUT   Q
      Why are you going?

(311) tutu   ʌngeik-ʌn   zor-iwa ni
      wool^bag sell-IMPF   go-INT CERT
      I'm going to sell wool bags.

The question word *azi* 'how?' deals with manner. The phrase *gʌggi reʔtos* in (312) is an idiom meaning 'reply' or 'answer'.

(312) azi   gʌggi reʔtos-ik-o
      how?   answer-OBL-Q
      How should I answer? *or* What should I say?

Most occurrences of *azi* that I have encountered are in indirect questions, as in (313).

(313) azi   niʔ-ni   neki   aʔzan-uʔ   nʌn-na
      what   do-CERT   CNTR   think-NEG   AUX-DIST
      He didn't know what to do.

When a question involves elements within a postpositional phrase, the postposition immediately follows the question word. In (314), *-ikin* (limitative) follows both the question word and the time word and indicates a time to which an action or state will continue.

(314) bin   zán   -ikin   nʌ-nʌ-ŋ-waʔk-ʌn-no
      when?   COP   LIM   2S-1O-BEN-look-IMPF-Q
      Until when will you wait for me?
      How long will you wait for me?

(315) biérne -kin   mi-ŋ-waʔk-ʌn   nʌ-ngua   ni
      Friday LIM   2O-BEN-look-IMPF   1O-FUT   CERT
      I will wait for you until Friday.

6.4–6.6 Imperatives

Imperatives involve a lexical verb followed by a stressed auxiliary verb. The lexical verb is either uninflected or carries *-uʔ* (negative) or *-ʌn* (imperfective). The auxiliary verb is inflected only for the future imperative *ú-nik-ža* (aux-when-medial). The hortatory form is marked by *-ʌndi* (hortatory).

6.4. Immediate imperatives. Sentence (316) illustrates a positive immediate imperative.

(316) *amase   ú*
      get^up   AUX
      Get up! *or* Stand up!

The auxiliary verb recieves heavy (phrase) stress. When the verb stem ends in an unstressed *a*, *u* (auxiliary) tends to be enclitic and the sequence *aú* becomes *óu*, as in (317) with the verb *guka* 'pick up'.

(317) *gukó-u*
      pick^up-AUX
      Pick it up!

Using the auxiliary *awa* rather than *u* indicates that an action is to be performed immediately but at a short distance from the place of the speech act.

(318) *awakati   dže   ido-awa*
      avocado   water   spill-AUX
      (Go) water the avocado tree (over there)!

In a negative imperative the auxiliary is *nʌn*.

(319) *tšoʔs-uʔ   nʌn*
      put^down-NEG   AUX
      Don't put it down!

When a verb carries *-ʌn* (imperfective), an action is to be performed over a span of time, and the auxiliary verb is *nuk* (with the *k* deleted word-finally). The implication is that the speaker is going away and will be back shortly, but the hearer should perform the action meanwhile.

(320) *mura   sia   ipas-ʌn   nú!*
      mule   saddle   put^on-IMPF   AUX
      Put the saddle on the mule!

In a stative clause, the stressed verb is the copula appropriate to the particular predicate adjective, as in *zʌn* (copula) with *te* 'quiet' and *nʌn* (copula) with *tin* 'still'.

(321) te   zʌ́n
      quiet COP
      Be quiet!

(322) gʌmmʌsini tin   nʌ́n
      boy   still COP
      Son, be still!

6.5. Future imperatives. A future imperative utilizes -*nik* 'when' and -*ž* (medial) to indicate that a hearer is to perform some action later. (*Besamano* 'kiss hand' is borrowed from Spanish.)

(323) besamano besamano ké-i-nik-ža
      greetings greetings PERI-say-when-MED
      Give him/her my greetings!

(324) akusa nʌ-n-zasó-u-nik-ža
      needle 1O-BEN-save-AUX-when-MED
      Save a needle for me!

A future imperative may combine with negative. The auxiliary verb used in this case is *nʌn*, as with an immediate imperative.

(325) džui   aʔtaʔnig-uʔ nʌ́n-nik-ža
      money loan-NEG   AUX-when-MED
      Don't loan out the money (in the future)!

A future imperative with -*ʌn* (imperfective) indicates that an action should be performed in the future over a span of time but before the speaker returns.

(326) buru   tak-ʌn   núʔ-nik-ža
      burro look^for-IMPF AUX-when-MED
      Look for the burro!

6.6. Hortatory. The hortatory is marked by -*ʌndi* (hortatory) on a lexical verb or on a following auxiliary.

(327) as-ʌndi
      sit-HORT
      Let's sit down!

(328) kʌnii mi   aw-ʌndi
      cane   grind AUX-HORT
      Let's grind sugar cane!

The force of the hortatory is to suggest or invite rather than to command. A person may use it with inceptive aspect, to suggest to others that they begin doing something. For example, (329) could be used when a group has met to discuss an action, and now it is time to begin.

(329) asái-m-pana   aw-ʌndi
      talk-IMPF-INCEP   AUX-HORT
      Let's begin to talk!

6.7. Negation. Negation is marked in the verb phrase by the suffix *-uʔ* (negative), which has the form *-ʔ* following a vowel-final morpheme.

(330) mura neki tšuza-ʔ   nar -i   -ri
      mule CNTR see-NEG   AUX while TOP
      He did not see the mule...

The negative occurs on the main verb of a clause, even when its scope is a subordinate verb in a merged complement. For example, in (331), the negative with *guaʔsa* (cause) negates the subordinate verb 'spray out' rather than *guaʔsa* itself.

(331) ši   wis-ʌn   neki guaʔs-uʔ   nar -i
      foul^odor   spray-IMPF   CNTR cause-NEG   AUX while
      She prevented the skunk's scent from spraying out (i.e., caused to not spray out)...

A second major function of the negative is to interact with the tag of a leading yes/no question in order to make the whole statement affirmative or negative (§6.2). If the lexical verb is negative as well as the tag, the whole statement is negative.

(332) mura neki tšuzan-uʔ na-ʔ   no
      mule CNTR see-NEG   COP-NEG   Q
      I don't see the mule, do I?

However, the lexical verb may be negative yet the whole statement positive if the tag is positive. In (333), the verb is negative with the negative carried by the optional auxiliary verb *aw* (reduced to *a*), and the tag is positive.

(333) *tigri   peri   mouga   nʌ-kʌ-gga   au-?   no*
       jaguar dog   two   1O-PERI-eat AUX-NEG Q
       The jaguar ate my two dogs (didn't it?)

Sentence (333) occurs in a context where it is clear that indeed the jaguar killed the dogs. Thus, in leading yes/no questions, negation on the lexical verb does not negate that verb, but indicates that the polarity of the proposition is that of the tag.

7
Sentence Formation

Clause chaining, a phenomenon common in SOV languages, provides the major mechanism for combining clauses into sentences in Ika (Givón 1984:71). Sentences are made up of one or more clauses. A nonfinal clause is marked for the logical or temporal relationship it has with the clause it precedes. In the discussion that follows, the suffixes that specify these relationships are termed CLAUSE CONNECTORS. They include both the notions of coordination and subordination. Final clauses are not marked for these relationships but have mood indicators for declarative, imperative, or interrogative (Givón 1984:70). The clause connectors are listed in (334). The conjunctions *pari* 'from', *nangua* 'and', and *guinti* 'finally' may follow *-i* 'while', *-eʔ* 'then', and *-adžu* (immediate succession).

(334) *-i*   'while'
       -eʔ   'then'
       -adžu (immediate succession)
       -ameʔ (cause)
       -ndi   (condition)

Clause connectors occur in the configuration 'X-z Y', where X and Y are two clauses and z is the clause connector. Any discussion of the two events connected by a clause connector has to do with the events referred to by X and Y, respectively.

SENTENCE INTRODUCERS provide a way to link two sentences by means of an auxiliary verb with deictic suffixes (§5.11) and a clause connector. The sentence introducer shows the relationship between the independent clause of the previous sentence and the first clause of the next sentence.

7.1. Temporal clause connectors. The connector *-i* 'while' specifies temporal overlap or inclusion, or that two events are tightly (but not causally) connected. The subject of a clause marked by *-i* is almost always the same as the subject of the next clause, as in (335).

(335) mouga máikʌnɨ hau hau zʌnʔ kʌ-dar   -i   -ri
     two   three   yip yip just PERI-bark while TOP

       perɨ te   nis -eʔ -ri
       dog   quiet do then TOP
     Barking two or three times, the dog became quiet, ...

The connector *-eʔ* 'then' indicates 'X and then Y' in either a logical or a temporal sense. With *-eʔ*, in contrast to *-i* 'while', the two connected events are more likely to involve a different subject, show temporal succession rather than overlap, and stand in a causal relationship. Sentence (336) illustrates *-eʔ* in a context that shows both temporal succession and a causal relationship.

(336) tigri   ʌnneki ʌn-tšuza-ʔ   nar -eʔ   nʌngua -ri
     jaguar CNTR   REF-see-NEG   AUX then   and   TOP

       eigui keiwɨ   tak-ʌn   zoža-na
       also   right^away   look^for-IMPF go-DIST
     They didn't see the jaguar, and then (so) they went to look for it again.

Sentence (337) shows a case with *-eʔ* involving a change of subject between clauses.

(337) eiki   ri-žun-ʌn   nus -eʔ   -ri   nʌngua -ri
     still 3pS-go^down-IMPF   AUX then TOP and   TOP

       perɨ -ri inʔgui eigui keiwɨ   zoža-na
       dog   TOP one   also   right^away go-DIST
     They were still going down, and then one dog took off.

-eʔ 'then' may also occur with *-nik* 'when' to mark a time-conditional relationship 'when X, then Y'. In (338), talking about how cable cars

operate in pairs, *-e?* indicates that the event indicated by the first clause temporally precedes that indicated by the second clause and *-nik* marks the first event as the condition under which the second event takes place.

(338) eikɨ itšun-nik-ž   -e? -ri, iwa eim -ekɨ zanɨ
       there go^up-when-MED then TOP now that LOC from

          ʌn-žunʌ-ž   -e? -ri
          REF-go^down-MED   then TOP
When it goes up, the one up there comes down...

The connector *-adžu* (immediate succession) indicates two events that follow immediately one after another, without temporal overlap, performed by the same subject.

(339) du   kaw -i   a?tʌrɨ u-n   -adžu nʌngua -ri
       good seem while skin   AUX-DIST -IMM   and   TOP

          du   kaw   -i   mantékɨ -se? isua aw   -i
          good seem while lard   LOC   cook AUX while
As soon as she skinned it well, she fried it in lard well...

In certain instances, a clause may have no clause connecting suffix yet be interpreted as part of a clause chain. Such cases involve one or more instances of the same verb, usually a motion verb, marked by *-na-ri* (distal-topic), the last verb being followed by *guinti* 'finally' or *nʌngua* 'and'. This combination of elements displays durativity—the action referred to took place over a span of time.

(340) ri-žun-na   -ri, žun-na   -ri, žun-na   -ri
       3pS-go^down-DIST TOP   go^down-DIST   TOP   go^down-DIST   TOP

          guinti   péri -se? kʌ-dan-ʌn   nuk-ž   -ekɨ mʌtšéi
          finally dog   ERG   PERI-bark-IMPF AUX-MED   LOC   near

          kʌtšar -e?   -ri
          arrive then TOP
They went down, down, down until finally they arrived near where the dog had barked at something...

One verb alone may signal durativity in this way, provided it carries *-na-ri guinti* (distal-topic finally) as in (341).

(341) ingiti sekʌnar-i žun-na   -ri guinti, ingí ziʔi
       little stalk-while go^down-DIST TOP finally little red

       tšu-ai   aʔzar -eʔ
       see-seems think then

He descended stalking carefully until finally he thought, "I can see a little red."

Frequently the two clauses joined in this way involve a motion verb followed by a verb indicating arrival, as in (342).

(342) ʌm-win-igeis   -i   ʌn-žun-na   -ri nʌngua -ri
       REF-3pS-put^up^on   while REF-go^down-DIST TOP and   TOP

       urakɨ -sikɨ kʌtšar -i   -ri
       house LOC   arrive while TOP

They descended carrying it and arrived at the house...

The conjunctions *pari* 'from' and *nʌngua* 'and' may occur with *-i* 'while', *-eʔ* 'then', and *-adžu* (immediate succession). *pari* 'from' indicates a change in episode or a turning point in a narrative. In a number of hunting stories, for example, if a hunter fails to find his quarry, gets scared, or does not know what to do, he leaves the scene, and this crucial point is marked by *pari*.

(343) Pedru -ri tšoutšo kʌnas -i   azi au-kua ni   neki
       Pedro TOP fear   have while what AUX-OBL CERT CNTR

       aʔzan-uʔ   guɨn nar -eʔ pari -ri tšoutšou kʌnas -eʔ
       think-NEG   ?   AUX then from TOP fear   have   then

       kure nika u-na
       run do   AUX-DIST

Pedro got scared and didn't know what to do, and from that point he got scared and he ran.

7.2. Logical clause connectors. The conjunction *-ameʔ* 'because' marks a clause as the CAUSE for the next clause.

(344) *semana santa džuia? -se? kʌ́nkʌnʌn nai-n zoža-na-ru*
week holy day LOC forest walk-IMPF go-DIST-1S

-ame? zʌn? tigri peri mouga nʌ-kʌ-gga au-? no
CAUS just jaguar dog two 1O-PERI-eat AUX-NEG Q
Because I went hunting in Holy Week, the jaguar ate my two dogs, didn't it.

The conjunction *-ndi* 'if' marks a clause as a CONDITION. A clause marked by *-ndi* may precede or follow the clause to which it refers.

(345) *husiri nʌ-kʌ-na -ndi tšaža ninza*
shotgun 1O-PERI-COP COND shoot 1RES
If I had my shotgun, I would shoot.

(346) *witš-u? ki nán-ak-o ʌndin zue -ndi*
die-NEG CNTR AUX-OBL-Q under go COND
Would you die if you went underneath?

Clause connectors that mark temporal relationships do not have this freedom because clause order is strictly iconic, determined by the order in which the events occurred.

7.3. Sentence introducers. An independent clause is not marked for its logical or temporal relationship to a following clause, as is a medial clause. A sentence introducer, however, contains the clause connectors and conjunctions which show how the final, independent clause of the previous sentence is related to the first clause of the sentence the introducer initiates. Especially within narrative, sentence introducers enable a speaker to break the grammatical clause-to-clause sequence while still indicating (by means of the sentence introducer) how actions are related to one another.

A sentence introducer is made up of *ei* 'thus' (a sort of pro-verb), followed by an auxiliary verb carrying deictic and clause-connecting suffixes, optionally followed in turn by one of the conjunctions *pari* 'from' or *nʌngua* 'and'. Sentences (347)-(349) are drawn from a single narrative. The sentence introducer at the beginning of (348) indicates temporal overlap between the actions of chasing (347) and climbing (348). The introducer at the beginning of (349) presents the actions of shooting (348) and killing (349) as a temporal sequence.

(347) ... inʔgui -seʔ zʌnʔ eiki was   -i   žun-na
         one   ERG   just   still chase while go^down-DIST
       One still went down chasing it.

(348) ei   aw   -i   nʌngua -ri   kʌn -seʔ keiwi   eigui
       thus AUX while and   TOP tree LOC   right^away also

       an-itšon-ʌn   nus -eʔ   nʌngua -ri   José -seʔ
       REF-go^up-IMPF   AUX then   and   TOP   José ERG

       eigui tšei-na
       also   shoot-DIST
       (While it was chasing the puma,) the puma climbed a tree, and
       then José shot.

(349) ei   u-ž   -eʔ   nʌngua guako-u-na
       thus AUX-MED then and   kill-AUX-DIST
       (He shot it, and then) he killed it.

A number of clause-chaining languages in Papua New Guinea also use
the first element of a sentence to provide linkage with a prior sentence.
"Commonly the function of the first base in such chaining units is to refer
back to the last base of the previous chain" (Longacre 1972:45; cf. also
Grimes 1972:521).

Occasionally, the first clause of a sentence repeats the last verb of the
preceding sentence, but with a different deictic suffix and a clause
connecting-suffix. This is in contrast to beginning with a sentence
introducer. The text above continues in (350) and (351). This repetition of
the lexical verb indicates a significant break in the flow of a narrative, in
this case the culmination of the hunt and the winding down of the story.

(350) ei   u-ž   -eʔ   nʌngua guako-u-na
       thus AUX-MED then and   kill-AUX-DIST
       And so he killed it.

(351) **guaka** aw   -i   -ri   gasiro   aʔkui   u-ž   -eʔ   -ri
       kill   AUX while TOP   intestines cut^out   AUX-MED then TOP

       mʌndongu -seʔ -ri   wimi   áikʌni sʌmmi k-ʌnikua-na
       stomach   LOC   TOP   meat   apart   lots   PERI-be^in-DIST
       Killing it, they gutted it, and there was a lot of meat in its
       stomach.

Kayapó of Brazil shows a similar phenomenon: "... the verbatim repetition of a verb which is final in one sentence as the verb which leads into the succeeding action in the next sentence" (Stout and Thomson 1971:254). Note that one use of such verbatim repetition of a verb is to indicate the change from introduction to plot and plot to coda in Kayapó narrative.

8
Subordination

Subordinate clauses in Ika fall into four catergories: relative clauses, locative nominalized clauses, clauses as complements of verbs, and adverbial clauses.

8.1. Relative Clauses. The basic strategy for forming a relative clause is to place a head noun in clause-initial position in a restricting clause having a nonfinite verb and to embed that restricting clause as one constituent of a matrix clause. There is no relative pronoun or evidence of gapping, given that variation in word order in main, declarative clauses makes it impossible to fix an invariable position for major clause constituents. Thus, it is impossible to say that a noun phrase has been MOVED, simply that it usually occurs in clause-initial position. When topic and case markers occur with a relative clause, they occur on the end of the restricting clause rather than on the head noun itself, suggesting that the head noun is internal to the relative rather than external. These characteristics are consistent with Comrie's discription of internally-headed relative clauses, in which "the head noun remains expressed with the relative clause, in the usual form for a noun of that grammatical relation within a clause, and there is no overt expression of the head in the main clause" (1981:138). Comrie also notes that internal heading is even clearer when the embedded clause, rather than the head noun itself, may take appropriate suffixes to indicate its role in the main clause (ibid).
 Most relative clauses encountered in text are relativizations into the subject position of the restricting clause, with the restricting clause

following the head noun.[33] Three examples in my data show relativization into object position, one with prenominal and two with postnominal restricting clause. One example shows relativization into the locative or indirect object. The verb phrase in a relative clause is nonfinite in that it lacks mood marking but is otherwise identical to the verb phrases of an independent clause.

Example (352) illustrates the most frequently occurring type of relative clause—relativization into the subject position. Notice the ergative and topic markers at the end of the relative clause (bracketed). If the head noun were a constituent of the matrix clause, I would expect these markers to occur on the noun rather than at the end of the restricting clause.

(352) [iki inʔgui Rísiu zaʔki nuk-ža] -seʔ -ri ʌn-tšua-na
     man one Lisio name COP-MED ERG TOP REF-see-DIST
     A man named Lisio saw it.

Not all examples of relative clauses show case or topic marking to help identify their status as an embedded clause. In (353), for example, the embedded clause occurs between a sentence-inital locative word and the verb at the end of the sentence. The declarative mood marker *ni* (certainty) pertains to the verb of the matrix clause, while the verb of the restricting clause has no such mood marking. In addition to carrying no mood indicator, the verb of the restricting clause is also apparently limited to a choice between only *-ža* (medial) or *-na* (distal).[34]

(353) džoʔsʌgaka [peri guiadžina wásʌ-ža] kuʌ-ža ni
     Yoʔsʌgaka dog puma chase-MED live-MED CERT
     A dog that chases pumas lives in Yoʔsʌgaka.

My corpus contains three clear cases of relativization into the object position, one with a prenominal restricting clause and two with a postnominal restricting clause. Example (354) of relativization into the

---

[33]The higher frequency of subject relatives is consistent with Comrie and Keenan's suggestion that, cross-linguistically, it is easier to relativize into the subject position. "In absolute terms subjects are the most relativizable of NPs" (Comrie and Keenan 1979:653). In this instance, the principle has a statistical rather than a categorical effect. Both subject and object relatives occur, but subject relatives are more common.

[34]The other deictic suffixes are used only with first and second person (§5.11), and this probably accounts for the fact that I have not observed them in relative clauses. It would be unusual for someone to say "I, who am..." or "you, who are..."

object position shows a prenominal restricting clause. SVO word order is quite rare in main clauses, but the most frequent pattern for forming relatives does not suggest gapping or movement of the head noun. Therefore I consider the head of the relative clause in (354) also to be internal to the restricting clause, except that here it occurs at the end of the restricting clause.

(354) *[guiadžina -seʔ ga-na tšiwa] -ri wanak-akí nuk-ž -abaʔ*
 puma ERG eat-DIST goat TOP bring-PRF AUX-MED LOC
 where (they) had brought the goat that the puma ate

In (355), *kʌn* 'stick' is the head noun and object of *ga* 'eat' in the postnominal restricting clause.

(355) *[kʌn zi -seʔ ga-na] dingíri kaw-in*
 stick worm ERG eat-DIST full^of^holes seem-WIT
 The stick that the worms ate is full of holes.

In (356), also involving a postnominal restricting clause, *gaʔkʌnamɨ* 'word' is the head noun and the object of *guk* 'pick up' in the restricting clause. Note that topic marking *(-ri)* comes at the end of the restricting clause rather than on the head noun itself.

(356) *[eima gaʔkʌnamɨ makina -seʔ guk-ʌn nuk-ža] -ri*
 this word machine LOC pick^up-IMPF AUX-MED TOP

 riwi-ʌn nuk-ža na-ʔ nʌn-no
 learn-IMPF AUX-MED AUX-NEG AUX-Q
 (They) are learning the words that they get out of the machine (tape recorder), aren't they?

When the NP of (356) is relativized into a locative or indirect object position, as in (357), *makina* 'machine' retains its case marking according to its role in the restricting clause (marked by *-seʔ* (locative)), and *-ri* (topic) remains at the end of the restricting clause, but *makina* appears in initial position in the restricting clause. The fact that *makina* is case marked for its role in the restricting clause while the topic marker occurs at the end of the restricing clause provides additional evidence that the head noun in such clauses is internal to the restricting clause.

(357) [*makina -seʔ gaʔkʌnamɨ guk-ʌn*   *nuk-ža]*   *-ri*
machine LOC word   pick^up-IMPF AUX-MED TOP

       grabadora   *auga ni*
       tape^recorder RPT CERT
The machine that they get words out of is called a tape recorder.

To summarize briefly, most relative clauses in text are relativizations into the subject position with a subject-initial, internally-headed restricting clause. Case and topic marking on the end of the restricting clause rather than on the head noun itself support such an analysis. Three examples of relativization into the object position show both postnominal and prenominal restricting clauses. The example of relativization into the locative, again, shows a postnominal restricting clause with topic-marking on the end of the restricting clause.

8.2. Locative nominalized clauses. The enclitic postpositions *-ekɨ* and *-abaʔ* may follow a clause-final verb with no mood marker to subordinate it to a following clause as in (358).

(358) [*perɨ zʌ-džua*   *papá zɨn*   *-ekɨ]*   *aʔtšun-na*   *-ri*
      dog GEN-blood flat   be   LOC   arrive-DIST TOP
He arrived where there was dog blood on the ground...

The deictic suffix *-na* (distal) is used in locative clauses to name the location of a past event.

(359) *ʌn-zoža-na*   [*tšinu ga-n*   *-ekɨ]*
      REF-go-DIST pig   eat-DIST LOC
He went to where (something) ate the pig.

The case marking postposition *-abaʔ* (locative) nominalizes a clause to name an area rather than a place or point. A number of examples involving *-abaʔ* have motion verbs in the embedded clause resulting in something like 'along where it went', as in (360).

(360) [*ʌn-zoža-n*   *-abaʔ]*   *ta*   *kingui eigui kʉsárɨ -ri*
      REF-go-DIST LOC straight same also deer   TOP

       ʌn-nak-ʌn   *nuʔ-na*
       REF-come-IMPF AUX-DIST
The deer came straight back by the same way it had gone.

Locative nominalized clauses may occur between main clause constituents, as any other locative element does.

(361) sʌbastian -di [kusari kʌ-zagi-n -abaʔ] itšon-ʌn
 Sebastian TOP deer PERI-pass-DIST LOC go^up-IMPF

 nus -eʔ -ri
 AUX then TOP
Sebastian went up to where the deer passed...

8.3-8.8 Complementation

There are several types of complementation in Ika, with a range of variation in how restricted the complement must be. That is, the complement may be completely unrestricted, as in a direct quotation where any valid utterance may serve as the complement to the quotative verb, while other main verbs require that their verbal complement carry a particular suffix, or no suffix at all. Some verbs of speaking and cognition take direct quotation complements, that is, the clauses which they take as complements could themselves stand as independent sentences. Other verbs take nonfinite complements (having a verb with no mood marking). Indirect questions form another type of complement, combining some features of declarative marking and other features of interrogative marking. Motion verbs take a verbal complement indicating the purpose of the motion; the embedded verb in such clauses has a restricted grammatical form. Verbs with a particular suffix may show resultant state, serving as the complement to a copula (e.g., 'he is gone' vs. 'he went'). The verb *aʔdžun* 'want' takes the most restricted complement—a verb which cannot have a suffix.

8.3. Verbs with full sentence complements. The verbs *aʔzan* 'think', *ža* 'say', and *auga* (reportative) take full sentences as quotative complements. There is no restriction on the complement It may be one sentence or more—declarative, imperative, or interrogative. The quotation is direct in the sense that it does not change according to the person quoting or the time when the quotation is made. The quotation is usually a regular utterance but may be an onomatopoeic word or a pro-quote such as *eimei* 'like this'. Example (362) has *ža* 'say' as the verb with its quotative complement.

(362) kʌ́nkʌnʌn   nai-n   zei-kua,   nʌ-kʌ-ža-n   -ame?
      forest   walk-IMPF   go-OBL   1O-PERI-say-DIST   CAUS
      Because he said to me, "Let's go hunting"...

The next two examples illustrate complements which are interrogative and imperative, respectively.

(363) tšua   me-ʔdžun-o   nʌ-ke-i   -eʔ   -ri
      see   2O-want-Q   1O-PERI-say   then TOP
      He said to me, "Do you want to see it?"...

(364) an-gó-u   kʌ-ža   -ri
      REF-do-AUX   PERI-say   TOP
      He said to him, "Do it!"...

Although the complement of a verb like *ža* 'say' is usually an actual or possible utterance, it may also be an onomatopoeic word, or an adverb, *ei* 'thus' or *eimei* 'like this', which stands in for a quotation whose content is known. An example of an onomatopoeic quotation is the word *pɨ* imitating the sound of an angry puma.

(365) guidžina -ri   pɨ pɨ, keiwɨ   ža-n
      puma   TOP   right^away   say-DIST
      The puma said, "*pɨ pɨ*."

eimei 'like this' may stand in for some actual quotation when the participants in the situation know what has been said, or the speaker is about to make a lengthy quotation, as when beginning to relate a story.

(366) José   eimei   i-n
      José   like^this   say-WIT
      José said it like this.

auga (reportative) also takes full sentence complements but is never inflected for person.

(367) tigri   guákʌ-ža anáʔnuga awʌnʔ kawa guákʌ-ža auga
      jaguar   kill-MED animal   big   seem kill-MED RPT

      guin na   -ndi
      ʔ   AUX COND
      Since they say, "It kills jaguars. It kills big animals," ...

8.4. Verbs with complements not marked for mood. The verbs *tšua* 'see', *ža* 'say', and *kawa* 'seem' take complements which are sentences lacking only mood indicators. The subject of the embedded verb is different from the subject of the main verb. Example (368) illustrates *tšua* 'see' with such an object complement.

(368) džuiaʔ -ri   naž-ʌn   nuk-ža   neki tšu-ʔ   na-rua   ni
      day   TOP   walk-IMPF   AUX-MED   CNTR see-NEG AUX-1S   CERT
      I have not seen it walk around in the daytime.

ža 'say' with a complement not marked for mood means 'make a sound like *x*' or 'it sounds like *x*'. The implication is that someone heard something happen, but *ža* 'say' is always inflected for third-person singular (i.e., unmarked), ruling out as an interpretation 'hear *x*'.

(369) dže   meina   -ki   kʌtšanʌ-ža   ža-na
      river stream LOC   arrive-MED   say-DIST
      It sounded as if it reached the stream.

The arguments of the embedded sentence are case marked for their role in the embedded sentence rather than the main sentence. In (370), for example, *peri* 'dog' receives the ergative marking appropriate for the subject of the embedded verb 'find'.

(370) peri -seʔ   kaʔtšonʌ-ža   keiwi   i
      dog   ERG   find-MED   right^away   say^while
      It sounded like the dog found it ...

kawa 'seem' takes a sentential complement as its only argument.

(371) mákʌri -seʔ   ga-na   kaw-in
      vulture ERG   eat-DIST   seem-WIT
      It seems that a vulture ate it.

kawa takes the mood marking of a regular verb but is not marked for person and is, in a sense, subjectless. Its usage shows that it means 'it seems to me', but, grammatically, it is not marked for first person. *kawa* is also used as a copula for constructing adjective and adverbial phrases. In (372), the first instance of *kawa* is copular while the second takes the preceding sentence as its complement. (*na? no* is a tag expecting a positive reply.)

(372) iwa   peibu -se?   -ri   diwʌn   kaw -i   tutusoma isʌ-ža
now   Kogi ERG TOP different seem while hat   SEW-MED

      kawa na-?   no
      seem AUX-NEG Q
Now it seems (to me) that the Kogis sew a different sort of hat.

A second use of *kawa* means 'have to X' and involves a complement marked by -*ikua* (obligation), with *kawa* taking an object prefix to refer to the person that has to do the action listed in the complement.

(373) ribru   mi-kʌ-ták-ikua   nʌ-kaw-in
book   2O-PERI-look^for-OBL 1O-seem-WIT
I have to hunt for your book.

The subject of the embedded verb is the same as the referent of the object marker on *kawa*.

8.5. Indirect questions. The verbs *a?zan* 'think (know)', *awan* 'not be sure', and *tšua* 'see' may take indirect question complements. There is no restriction on whether or not the subject of the indirect question is the same as the subject of the main verb. An indirect yes/no question has the same form as an independent yes/no question yet serves as the complement to a main verb which may take an indirect question complement.

(374) džuia? kure nik-ʌn-no awán-ʌkuei
day   run   do-IMPF-Q   not^sure-ABLE
I am uncertain whether they run around in the daytime or not.

Indirect content questions work somewhat differently. These complements have a question word yet take declarative mood marking (*ni* (certainty) or suffix -*in* (witness)). *a?zan* 'think' frequently appears with the negative to mean 'not know', with an indirect content question complement, as in (375).

(375) ini   ni   neki   wina-ʔza-ʔ   na
      what? CERT CNTR   3pO-think-NEG   AUX
      They didn't know what it was.

(376) illustrates *aʔzan* in the absence of a negative word.

(376) azi   u-niʔ-ku-e   keiwi   aʔzan-ʌn   nuʔ-n   -adžu
      how?   AUX-when-MED-Q   right^away   think-IMPF   AUX-DIST   IMM
      As soon as she knew what she would do...

I have encountered one example of *tšua* 'see' with an indirect question complement.

(377) ini   pa   na   keiwi   win-tšu-ž   -eʔ   nʌngua
      what? flat be   right^away   3pIS-see-MED   then   and
      They saw something lying down...

8.6. Motion verbs with purpose complements. Verbs of motion may take a complement whose verb is marked only by *-ʌn* (imperfective), indicating 'go in order to *x*'. The subject of the embedded verb must be the same as the subject of the motion verb, the two actions being closely connected. In (378), the 'shooting' occurs at the place where the 'going' ends.

(378) monu   tšai-n   ʌn-zoža-na
      monkey   shoot-IMPF   REF-go-DIST
      He went (in order) to shoot monkeys.

Purpose may also be expressed with two clauses when the two events involved are less-closely related. In (379), the first clause expresses purpose, indicated by the modal *-nguasi* (purpose), and the second clause the event prompted by the purpose. Note that the 'grinding' does not take place where the mule is found. One action is the purpose for another, but there is no requirement that the one action take place where the other action ends.

(379) kʌnii   mus-ʌn-guasi,   mura   ʌn-kʌ-taʔ-na
      cane   grind-IMPF-PURP   mule   REF-PERI-look^for-DIST
      He looked for the mule in order to grind sugar cane.

The enclitic modals -*ngua* (future) and -*nguasi* (purpose) (§9) take a purpose complement. Both constructions involve a verb marked by -*ʌn* (imperfective) followed by a verb which is temporally prior to the first verb (i.e., in 'go to look for', 'go' precedes 'look for' in time, and in 'will go', the intention precedes the 'going'). Compare (380) and (381).

(380) kʌniɨ   mus-ʌn   nʌ-ngua   ni
      cane   grind-IMPF   1O-FUT   CERT
      I will grind sugar cane.

(381) kʌniɨ   mus-ʌn   zoža-na-rua   ni
      cane   grind-IMPF   go-DIST-1S   CERT
      I went (in order) to grind sugar cane.

The causative verb *guaʔs* (§5.12) is also structurally similar to a motion verb with a purpose complement in that the embedded sentence has a verb marked only by -*ʌn* (imperfective). The subject of *guaʔs* (cause) and the subject of the embedded verb must be different, however, in contrast to purpose complements.

(382) apau   iniki   -seʔ   kʌ-nak-ʌn   neki   guaʔs-uʔ   neika
      owner   anyone   ERG   PERI-come-IMPF   CNTR   cause-NEG   FOC
      It does not let anything come near its owner.

8.7. Resultant state complements. A verb marked only by -*na* (distal) may serve as a complement to *zan*, a copular verb, to express the state resulting from an action. (383) illustrates a resultant state complement with the verb *zoža* 'go'.

(383) guidžina   -ri   ʌn-zoža-ná   zi-na
      puma   TOP   REF-go-DIST   COP-DIST
      The puma was gone.

With a transitive verb in the resultant state complement, the subject of the main clause is the object of the embedded clause.[35]

---

[35]Comrie 1981:112-13 discusses the resultative construction as an instance of natural ergative-absolutive syntax. That is, in constructions involving resultant state, many languages show patterns in which the participant in focus is either the subject of an intransitive verb or the object of a transitive verb, irrespective of whether the language is considered to be basically nominative-accusative or ergative-absolutive.

(384) tšinu   ga-ná   zar   -i   -ri
      pig   eat-DIST   COP   while   TOP
      The pig was eaten...

The resultant state complement differs both from a regular statement of an event in the past and from an anterior past (had done). (385) contrasts an event in the past, as a perfect (anterior past), and as a resultant state. *-na* on the embedded verb also supports an analysis of this construction as a complement to the copula rather than as a compound tense. Deictic suffixes may occur only once in a verb phrase, and as (385) shows, the copula may be marked for deictic aspect.

(385) Past
      guiadžina   zoža-na
      puma   go-DIST
      The puma went.

      Perfect
      guidžina   zož-akí   nuʔ-na
      puma   go-PRF   AUX-DIST
      The puma had gone.

      Resultant State
      guiadžina   zoža-ná   zɨ-na
      puma   go-DIST   COP-DIST
      The puma was gone.

8.8. *aʔdžun* 'want'. The verb *aʔdžun* 'want' takes the most restricted complement of the complement-taking verbs, namely a completely uninflected verb.

(386) tšua   na-ʔdžun-ni
      see   1O-want-CERT
      I want to see it.

To negate a construction, with *aʔdžun*, the matrix verb takes the negative suffix, the only element that may come between the two verbs being *au*, apparently an uninflected auxiliary verb, as in (388). Note that the participant referenced by the object prefixes on *aʔdžun* must be the same as the subject of the verb in the complement.³⁶

(387) *džoʔ -ri tšua aʔdzun-uʔ nʌn-na ni*
tail TOP see want-NEG AUX-DIST CERT
It didn't want to see the tail.

(388) *waʔka au me-ʔdžun-o*
look AUX 2O-want-Q
Do you want to look at it?

8.9. Adverbial clauses of simultaneous action. Adverbial clauses with a verb marked by *-i* 'while' indicate a simultaneously occurring action. The subject of the verb in the adverbial clause must be the same as the subject of the main verb; the subject noun phrase is case marked for its role in the embedded clause.

(389) *peri -seʔ -ri win-was -i žun-na*
dog ERG TOP 3pS-chase while go^down-DIST
The dogs went down chasing it.

Although the main verb is usually a motion verb, this is not a requirement. In (390), the main verb is *guak* 'kill'.

(390) *guiadžina zʌ-gʌmmi peri -seʔ anʌ-kuss -i*
puma GEN-child dog ERG REF-bite while

   guak-akí nuʔ-na.
   kill-PRF AUX-DIST
The dog had killed the baby puma, biting it.

---

³⁶The gloss 'want' for *aʔdžun* is actually somewhat misleading. The person 'wanting' is referenced as the object of a verb in the verb morphology, and the thing 'wanted' is presumably the subject. Thus a literal translation of *dže na-ʔdžun-ni* (water 1O-want-certainty) is something like 'Water is desirable to me'. This struck me as odd until Adolfo Constenla pointed out that this is parallel to Spanish verbs such as *gustar* 'like' which reference an experiencer as object of the verb (e.g. *El agua me gusta* 'I like water' or 'Water pleases me'). A number of other verbs follow this pattern, e.g. *kanan* 'own' (literally 'pertain to') and *aʔzun* 'swallow' (literally 'go down one's throat'). In all of these cases, the more animate participant is usually the object and the less animate participant is the subject.

Because -*i* 'while' is also used in clause chaining to show that the actions in two successive clauses temporally overlap, it is sometimes difficult to determine whether a particular fragment of speech represents two clauses in sequence or an adverbial clause. In clear cases of adverbial clauses, the embedded verb and the main verb occur immediately adjacent to each other, without intervening material; or the medial clause final enclitic -*ri* (topic) indicates two clauses in sequence. Example (391) shows a medial clause with -*i*. Note that the first clause ends in -*rɨ* (topic) and a noun comes between the two verbs.

(391) mouga máikʌnɨ hau hau zʌnʔ kʌ-dar -i -ri
 two three yip yip just PERI-bark while TOP

 perɨ te nis -eʔ -ri
 dog quiet do then TOP
 Barking at it two or three times, the dog got quiet ...

The enclitic -*i* 'while' is also used to form a second kind of adverbial phrase or clause in which constructions of the form NOUN COPULA-*i* indicate 'like a NOUN', as in (392). Such adverbial clauses may serve as predicate adjectives, as in (393).

(392) perɨ nar -i o aʔzɨna ni
 dog COP while mad think CERT
 It gets mad like a dog (does).

(393) gei nar -i kawa nin umaʔ -ri
 fire COP while COP CERT eye TO?
 (When you shine a light on it,) the eyes are like (i.e., shine like) a fire.

9
Pragmatics

This section discusses topics of a pragmatic nature: the handling of nonreferential and impersonal subjects; the function of *-seʔ* (ergative) in reflecting pragmatic factors governing zero anaphora and alternate word orders; two focus particles; and the pragmatic organization of clauses, including consideration of zero anaphora, the enclitic *-ri* (topic), the linear order of clause constituents, the system of participant reference, and the use of optional auxiliary verbs.

9.1. Nonreferential subjects. A construction involving a verb plus the copula *zan* indicates that the subject is nonreferential, that no particular or specific entity is being referred to. In (394), the speaker indicates that 'one can see' all of Bogotá from a certain vantage point. Although the speaker had the experience himself, he conveys the event as anyone would experience it.

(394) *Bogotá eima urakɨ -ri   kinki -ri   žóu-kɨtšɨ*
     Bogotá this   house TOP   really TOP   all-EMPH

     zʌnʔ tšu   zar-in
     just see   COP-WIT
     You see all the houses in Bogotá.

In (395), the same speaker discusses how people care for a garden. The scene is presented as not referring to any particular person.

(395) dže   dos   -i   átšu-ža   zar-in
     water spill while care^for-MED   COP-WIT
     Watering it, they care for it.

The second person singular *mi-* object prefix is also sometimes used nonreferentially. In (396), a hunter conveys that he cannot tell what it is that he is seeing, and uses a nonreferential 'you'.

(396) ini   ni   neki   me-ʔza-ʔ   nán-ʌkua   kau-ʔ   no
     what? CERT CNTR   2O-think-NEG AUX-OBL seem-NEG   Q
     It seems that you (one) can't tell what it is, doesn't it?

9.2. Off-stage subjects. The verb suffix *-kuma* (impersonal) serves to indicate that the subject of a clause, though referential, is not currently on stage, in the sense of participants being in focus at a given point in time. Often, the subject in such clauses is not among the regular 'cast' of a narrative, but performs an action which affects one of the participants. For example, (397) provides background information at the height of the action of a certain narrative: the shotgun shell which fails to fire is one previously given to the hunter by an unidentified party.

(397) inʔgui   kartutšu   aʔwe-kuma-na   gui   nʌn-na
     one   shell   give-IMPER-DIST   also be-DIST
     A shotgun shell had been given to him.

The participant which *-kuma* references may be part of the cast of characters in a narrative but temporarily out of focus. In one story, certain hunters split up into two groups, and one group becomes focal. During this part of the story, the nonfocal group is referenced by *-kuma*, as in (398).

(398) amʌse ʌw-in   amʌse ʌw-in   ke-i-kuma-ž   -eʔ   -ri
     get^up AUX-WIT   get^up AUX-WIT PERI-say-IMPER-MED   then   TOP
     "It got up. It got up," was being said to them, ...

Speakers sometimes use *-kuma* (impersonal) for first or second person plural subject in elicited forms. For example, in response to a request for the equivalent of 'we saw it', two forms may be given; (399) shows the first or second plural subject prefix while (400) has *-kuma* (impersonal) instead.

(399) *a-tšua   u-ž-in*
     12pS-see AUX-MED-WIT
     We saw it.

(400) *tšua   u-kuma-ž-in*
     see   AUX-IMPER-MED-WIT
     We saw it. (or possibly 'It was seen.')

In summary, *-kuma* (impersonal), makes reference to some unidentified, nonfocal participant(s) as subject.

9.3. Ergative marking of agent noun phrases. As has been noted previously (§1.14 and §4.1), agent noun phrases are marked by *-seʔ* (ergative) when the noun phrase occurs contiguous to the verb. (All the examples in this section are of transitive clauses and all references to SUBJECT here can be treated as equivalent to AGENT.) The subject noun phrase appears next to the verb when there is no overt object noun phrase (resulting in the order sv) and when the subject, object, and verb occur in other than the canonical sov order (osv, svo, ovs; cf. §9.6). Ergative marking is thus directly a result of surface word order, presumably functioning to disambiguate the roles of noun phrases, and is indirectly a result of the pragmatic conditions that control zero anaphora and alternate word orders.

In transitive clauses having the order sov, the subject receives no special case marking.

(401) Subject   Object Verb
     Gʌriwieri tigri   aʔwasa-na
     Gabriel   jaguar chase-DIST
     Gabriel went after a jaguar.

When the subject noun phrase appears contiguous to the verb, however, it is marked by *-seʔ* (ergative).

(402) Subject   Verb
     tigri   -seʔ   ʌn-ga-na
     jaguar ERG   REF-eat-DIST
     A jaguar ate it.

The potential ambiguity in role of a noun phrase can be clearly seen in example (413), in which a noun phrase occurs with the same verb in two clauses, once as object, once as subject. I was talking to two men about a painting of some pheasants, and, as neither the picture nor my explanation were clear to them, one of the men asked me the following, where the ergative marker makes clear the role of *ikɨ* 'person' as subject in the second clause.

(403)   Object   Verb   Subject   Verb
        ikɨ   *gʌ-ža,*   *kua*   *ikʌ*   *-seʔ*   *gʌ-ža*
        person eat-MED or   person ERG eat-MED
        They eat people or people eat them?

When an object appears postverbally, and a subject appears before the verb, the subject takes *-seʔ*.

(404)   Subject   Verb   Object
        Ruka   *-seʔ*   *-ri*   *sei ichua-na*   *José*
        Lucas   ERG   TOP   divine-DIST   José
        Lucas divined for José.

Ergative marking also occurs with OSV word order.

(405)   Object   Subject   Verb
        guiadžina zʌ-gʌmmɨ   *perɨ -seʔ*   *an-aʔkuss-i*   *guak-akí nuʔ-na*
        puma   GEN-child   dog   ERG   REF-bite   while   kill-PRF   AUX-DIST
        The dog had killed the puma's cub, biting it.

A postverbal subject is also ergative marked.

(406)   Object   Verb   Subject
        máikanɨ perɨ -ri   *kʌ-ga-na*   *guiadžina -seʔ -ri*
        three   dog   TOP   PERI-eat-DIST   puma   ERG   TOP
        The puma ate his three dogs.

One environment in which agent noun phrases are not usually marked as ergative is in clauses involving first- or second-person subject or object, even when a subject noun phrase occurs contiguous to the verb. In (407), the subject noun phrase comes immediately before the verb, but because the object is a second person (as shown by the prefix *mi-*), the subject is not marked by *-seʔ*. (408) illustrates a first-person pronoun as subject without *-seʔ*, even though it is in an immediately preverbal position. Clauses involving first or second person have clear indications in verb morphology of whether that participant is subject or object, and there is therefore no need to overtly mark the role of the subject noun phrase.

(407) Subject   Verb
      tigri   *mi-ga*
      jaguar   2O-eat
      The jaguar eats you.

(408) Subject   Verb
      nʌʔʌn -di   *tšu-ʔ*   *na-rua ni*
      1   TOP   see-NEG   AUX-1S CERT
      I did not see it.

Ergative marking always also occurs in one context in which the clause appears to have an SOV order. Clauses with embedded adverbial clauses may contain both a transitive and an intransitive verb, with both verbs sharing the same subject (§8.9). The intransitive verb is usually the main verb, and the subject noun phrase is marked as ergative to show that it is also the agent of the embedded transitive verb. In (409), the phrase *mouga neika* 'two of them' is the subject of both verbs, but *zoža* 'go' is the main verb of the clause while *was* 'chase' appears in a dependent form. The ergative marker on the subject noun phrase shows that it is an agent as well as the subject of *zoža* 'go'.

(409) Subject   Object   Verb
      mouga neika -seʔ *nʌngua guiadžina* *win-was -i*   *zoža-na*
      two   FOC   ERG   and   puma   3pS-chase while go-DIST
      Two of them went chasing the puma.

Tracy and Levinsohn (1977) have investigated the function of *-seʔ* in expository discourse. Their analysis revolves around the concepts of grammatical paragraphs and the thematic participant of the paragraph (usually the central character of the discourse). When some participant other than the central character "occupies the subject role within the paragraph, he is, as it were, displacing the central character from that role, and as such has to be marked with the suffix *-seʔ* (change of role)" (Tracy and Levinsohn 1977:7).

This analysis does not distinguish between the subject of transitive and intransitive verbs, which is a basic factor determining the occurrence of *-seʔ*, but it does give a clue to the circumstances in which the subject of a transitive clause is likely to occur next to the verb. In discourse, Ika shows a basic pattern in which known participants are not referenced by noun phrases whereas new participants must be specifically mentioned (see also §9.8). Thus, when some participant other than the central character is mentioned in the discourse as the subject of a transitive clause, it is referred to by a noun phrase which may appear next to the verb and will therefore be marked by -*se?*.

Ika provides additional data for judging competing cross-linguistic explanations of split ergativity. Comrie holds that agent noun phrases are marked as ergative when they do not make good agents—when, for example, the subject is nonhuman or inanimate while the object is human or animate. The expectation is that human or animate entities (as subject) act on nonhuman or inanimate entities (as object). When this normal expectation is reversed and the subject is less animate than the object, the subject must be specially marked, resulting in an ergative pattern. Comrie notes that one common cross-linguistic pattern is that "the ergative case is restricted to noun phrases that are low in animacy" (1981:123). Only in a limited sense does Ika follow this pattern. The animacy hierarchy usually places first and second persons (speech act participants) higher on the scale of animacy than third persons, and indeed, Ika does not mark as ergative first- and second-person pronouns but does mark third-person pronouns. However, this distinction clearly has nothing to do with animacy per se or with agentivity, but simply reflects the fact that many languages do treat speech act participants and third person differently.

Ika does, however, exemplify one type of language which Comrie identifies (1981:123):

> We should note that there are some languages where the occurrence of the special ergative or accusative marker is conditioned not by any specific rigid cut-off point on the animacy or definiteness hierarchies, but rather by a more general condition of the kind: use the special marker only if there is a likelihood of confusion between A[gent] and P[atient]; the assessment of likelihood of confusion is left to the speaker in the particular context.

Ergative marking of agent noun phrases in Ika follows a similar principle of using -*se?* only when there would be confusion between agent and patient, but this does not explain the pattern in any principled way.

DeLancey, by contrast, explains ergative patterns in terms of the two concepts VIEWPOINT and ATTENTION FLOW (DeLancey 1981). By attention flow DeLancey means "the flow of attention involved in actually witnessing the event" (1981:632) and holds that in transitive sentences, natural attention flow is from agent to patient. Viewpoint concerns the way in which the speaker chooses to describe an event, focusing on one or another participant in the event or choosing an external viewpoint as an uninvolved observer. DeLancey argues that in a transitive sentence, the agent is naturally the viewpoint. His explanation for ergative marking in a split ergative language is that "ergative case marking labels the starting point when it is not also the viewpoint; when the viewpoint and the starting-point coincide, the NP is not marked for case" (DeLancey 1981:653).

DeLancey's argument more closely matches the pattern of split ergativity with transitive verbs in Ika. The agent is the starting point of attention flow, and the viewpoint in general is the first of two noun phrases or the participant in the action which is absent (implicit) in the sentence. The discussion above shows that ergative marking occurs primarily in cases where the object is the implicit participant rather than the subject or when the object noun phrase precedes the subject, that is, when the starting point (the agent) is not also the viewpoint.

9.4. Focus. Two focus particles are *neki* (contrary to expectation) and *neika* (NP focus). Because contrast frequently involves what unexpectedly did not happen, most clauses containing *neki* are negative. In (410) 'I went to look for my mule' establishes the expectation that the man will find his mule, contradicted in (411). Note that the two clauses have the same subject and same object, but that the action itself in (411) is the unexpected result.

(410) *mura*   ʌn-kʌ-tak-ʌn   *zoža-na-rua*
      mule   REF-PERI-look^for-IMPF go-DIST-1S
      I went to look for my mule.

(411) *mura   neki   tšuza-ʔ   nar   -i   -ri*
      mule   CNTR   see-NEG   AUX   while   TOP
      I didn't see the mule...

Especially in cases where there is a change of subject from one clause to the next, *neki* occurs just before the negated verb but may also appear at the beginning of the clause to contrast the whole proposition with the expectation. In (422), the hunter expects his gun to fire but it does not; *neki* occurs at the beginning of the second clause as well as before the negated verb.

(412) *tšei-wa   aʔzar -eʔ   neki   husiri   neki   k-aʔwi-uʔ   nʌn-na*
      shoot-INT think then CNTR   shotgun CNTR   PERI-fire-NEG AUX-DIST
      He thought, "I'll shoot;" but his shotgun didn't go off.

The concept CONTRARY TO EXPECTATION, however, is not necessarily linked to negation. In some cases, two clauses are contrasted even when negation is not involved. In (413), for example, the first clause sets up an expectation that the hunter will go to see his shotgun-trap, but by contrast he gets scared and goes instead to ask for help in tracking his quarry.

(413) asigeʔ   husiri   tšu-ʌn   zor-iza   neki   tšoutšo   kʌnas   -eʔ
      next^day   shotgun   see-IMPF   go-RES   CNTR   fear   have   then

       pari -ri   Džonoʔsuí   keiwɨ   gaʔ-ž-ʌn   zoža-na
       from TOP   Donachuí   right^away   message-say-IMPF   go-DIST
       He wanted to go (would have gone) the next day to see the shotgun but instead he got scared and went to Donachuí to talk about it.

Just as *neki* (contrary to expectation) may occur in the absence of the negative, so negation may occur in contexts not involving contrast. That is, the expectation may be that the event will not or did not happen. This is the case where the same event is mentioned twice, both with the negative. The first mention often involves *neki* while the second mention does not. In (414), the statement 'we did not eat it' occurs twice (with two clauses in between but not given here), the first time in a contrastive context and the second time merely as repetition, without *neki*.

(414) ʌnneki   an-a-g-uʔ-nʌ́n   u-na
      CNTR   REF-12pS-eat-NEG-AUX   AUX-DIST

       ...eima kusári -ri   an-a-g-uʔ-nʌ́n   u-na   ni
       that deer   TOP   REF-12pS-eat-NEG-AUX   AUX-DIST   CERT
       We did not eat it... we did not eat that deer.

Another contrastive element (also sometimes occurring with the negative) is *neika* (NP focus). *neika* selects one item out of a set, either by way of contrasting two items or indicating which one is intended out of the available possibilities. In (415), *neika* occurs twice, in both cases to focus on certain dogs out of a pack.

(415) perɨ   umʌn   reʔmasi   neika -ri   aʔnɨ   win-was   -i   iwa
      dog   more   group   FOC   TOP   rock   3pS-chase while   now

       mouga   neika -seʔ   nʌngua   guiadžina   win-was   -i   zoža-na
       two   FOC   ERG   and   puma   3pS-chase while   go-DIST
       Most of the dogs chased the rocks (tumbling down the hillside), but two of them went chasing the puma.

In some cases, *neika* occurs with the negative to set up a double contrast, i.e. 'item-1 verb' versus 'item-2 not-verb'. For instance, in (416), the double contrast is 'eats ripe things' versus 'does not eat raw things'.

(416) *kuʔnana gʌ-ža   ni*
        ripe   eat-MED   CERT

   atšʌkai nar -i   g-uʔ   gui   neika ni
   raw   COP while eat-NEG   also   FOC   CERT
   It eats ripe fruit. It does not eat raw fruit.

9.5–9.9 The pragmatics of clause organization

Zero anaphora, linear order, the topic marker *-ri*, principles of participant reference, and optional auxiliary verbs all have to do with the pragmatic organization of the Ika clause. Zero anaphora—no overt noun phrase or pronoun reference to a participant in discourse—is statistically the most common means for referring to entities in connected speech. There tends to be relatively little variation in word order per se, with different combinations of present and absent clause constituents providing most of the variety in the linear organization of elements in clauses. Noun phrases that do occur, and clauses as a whole, may be marked by the enclitic *-ri* (topic) to indicate their special pragmatic status, with noun phrases marked in this way usually located in clause-initial position. Zero anaphora, unmarked noun phrases, and noun phrases marked by *-ri* provide the three basic choices in the system of participant reference in discourse.[37] The pragmatic topic-comment structuring of clauses also interacts with optional auxiliary verbs such that when the comment portion of a clause consists of only the verb phrase, that phrase is more likely to contain an auxiliary verb, giving the phrase a pragmatically marked structure.

9.5. Zero anaphora. In text, zero anaphora is the most common means of participant reference, with the result that the majority of clauses lack an overt noun phrase reference to the subject or object. It is, thus, not

---

[37]PARTICIPANT REFERENCE is here defined (§9.8) as encompassing cases of zero anaphora, where an entity is not overtly referenced in a clause but is part of the case frame of the verb.

uncommon to find clauses such as (417), in which neither subject nor object is referenced by an overt noun phrase.

(417) *guaka   u-na*
      kill   AUX-DIST
      He killed it.

In one collection of narrative and expository text, the overall rate of zero anaphora is 64.95%[38] Zero anaphora is significantly more common, however, with subjects than with objects. (418) compares zero anaphora for transitive subjects and objects in this same collection of texts.

(418) Zero anaphora for transitive subjects and objects

	Subjects	Objects
present	61	122
absent	177	116
zero anaphora	74.37%	48.74%
chi-square 33.0		

The results are not surprising, given that zero anaphora, in general, indicates the topicality of a participant, and that the grammatical category SUBJECT, is often associated cross-linguistically with the pragmatic category TOPIC. Thus subjects, naturally more topical, are more likely to be referenced by the topic-indicating device of zero anaphora.

The rate of zero anaphora for subjects of transitives and of intransitives is not significantly different, as the figures in (419) indicate.

(419) Zero anaphora for transitive and intransitive subjects.

	Intransitive	Transitive
present	83	61
absent	200	177
zero anaphora	70.67%	74.37%
chi-square 0.88; p greater than .10		

---

[38]493 of 759 instances of participant reference with no overt noun phrase or pronoun realization.

In general, zero anaphora represents the usual means of reference to a participant which figures in a series of clauses and may be treated as given information and topical.

9.6. The linear order of clause constituents. Data on the linear order of clause constituents indicate that Ika is basically verb-final and that subject precedes object when both constituents occur, although only ten percent of the transitive clauses are, strictly speaking, sov. (420) gives information on the linear order of elements in intransitive and transitive clauses.

(420) Word-order statistics

Transitive clauses		Intransitive clauses	
v	88	v	200
ov	89	sv	83
sv	28		
sov	23		
osv	3		
svo	3		
ovs	4		
Total	238	Total	283

Intransitive clauses are overwhelmingly subjectless, but all cases of noun-phrase subjects occur preverbally. Only 6.6% of transitive clauses with a noun-phrase subject show a postverbal subject (4 of 61) and only 2.5% of object noun phrases are postverbal (3 of 122). Ika is, thus, strongly verb-final.

Due to the high rate of zero anaphora, only 33 transitive clauses of 238 provide evidence concerning the relative order of subject and object.[39] Two-thirds of these clauses show sov order (23/33, or 69.70%). About half of the instances of sov clauses occur at beginnings, in the opening clauses of stories, where participants are first mentioned in a text or are reintroduced after an extended absence, and in isolated clauses in quoted

---

[39]The lower rate of verb-only clauses among transitives as opposed to intransitives is presumably due to the greater potential for confusion when both subject and object of a transitive clause are absent. Since zero anaphora for subjects is approximately the same for transitives and intransitives, while that for objects is lower, it may be that objects are chosen more often for explicit noun phrase reference in order to prevent this confusion.

speech. All of these circumstances show a great deal of discontinuity with the preceding context, requiring noun phrases to make reference clear.

The small number of clauses showing orders other than sov offer little opportunity to investigate motivations for these alternative orders, but a number of the examples of postverbal subjects occur in last mentions of a participant in a text.

9.7. -*ri* (topic). Tracy and Levinsohn (1977) list three functions for the enclitic -*ri*, one of the most frequently occurring morphemes in Ika.

a. to signal progression.

> The suffix -*ri* may occur as the last suffix in a non-final clause, signalling progression along the chronological or logical linkage axis of the backbone of the discourse... [-*ri* makes] the action of the following clauses a new and distinct event of the backbone. Its absence indicates lack of progression along the backbone, and a consequent bundling of the actions of the following clause(s) with the previous ones (1977:5).

b. to signal contrast when attached to adjectives

c. to signal a thematic participant

> One participant is selected to be the thematic participant of each paragraph. This is indicated by the suffix -*ri*, attached to the final word of the noun phrase which refers to the participant (1977:6).

After reviewing these three functions, I will suggest that, at the most general level, -*ri* serves to topicalize an element—to set off a clause, adjective, or noun phrase from surrounding material for pragmatic reasons.[40]

Separating distinct events. Approximately two-thirds of the examples of -*ri* in my data occur at the end of nonfinal clauses. Tracy and Levinsohn mention this use of -*ri* as indicating progression along the backbone of a discourse. When -*ri* occurs at the end of a nonfinal clause, the next clause is interpreted as a new and distinct event on the backbone of the discourse. In this environment, -*ri* follows the verb phrase of a nonfinal clause or the sentence introducer which begins a new sentence (§7.3). The

---

[40]The earliest known reference to -*ri* proposed that it marked pronouns as masculine (Isaacs 1884:184).

following examples each contain one sentence. (421) ends with *-ri*, indicating that 'the puma climbed a tree' is a distinct event on the storyline from the 'José fired again' of (422). The sentence introducer in (422), however, does not carry *-ri*, indicating that 'José shot' and the 'he killed it' of (423) are associated without progression along the event line.

(421) *ei   aw   -i   nʌngua -ri,   kʌn   -seʔ   eigui an-itšon-ʌn*
     thus AUX while and   TOP   tree   LOC   again REF-go^up-IMPF

     nus   -eʔ   nʌngua -ri
     AUX   then   and   TOP
(The puma) climbed a tree, and then

(422) *José eigui keiwɨ   tšei-na*
     José again right^away   shoot-DIST
José fired again.

(423) *ei   u-ž   -eʔ   nʌngua   guako-u-na*
     thus AUX   then   and   kill-AUX-DIST
And he killed it.

Most cases in narrative involving *-ri* at the end of clauses seem to serve this function of pragmatically separating two clauses which are to be considered distinct events. The clauses which are not separated by *-ri* likewise often show a lack of progression along the event line rather than distinct actions. Some clauses grouped together by the lack of *-ri* involve repetition, such as 'he went to look for the puma; he went up to Timaʔka, and 'He killed it. Having killed it...' Other cases involve two aspects of a single event, such as 'He went down; he arrived,' and 'José shot it; he killed it.' Still other groups of clauses involve description rather than events: 'Blood dripped out of its mouth, and it just stood there' and 'Its stomach had lots of meat in it. This they gave to the dogs.'

    Some aspects of the grouping or separating of clauses by *-ri* do not make as much sense in terms of this analysis, however. For example, the context for one of the examples given in the last paragraph contains three clauses which appear to be essentially all repetitions of the same event, yet the use of *-ri* at the end of the second clause groups the first two as separate from the third:

(424) He went to look for the puma. He went up to Tima?ka.

He went up to where the goat that the puma had killed had just been brought.

Again, in the same hunting story in which 'blood dripped out of its mouth' and 'it just stood there' are grouped together, 'the puma just stood there' and 'its tongue was hanging down' are not. These apparent contradictions suggest that this use of -*ri* is not so much a rule of grammar as a resource available to speakers to control the flow and pace of a narrative or other discourse. Thus, the grouping of clauses not only reflects principles such as repetition, description, and stages in a single event but also reflects the speaker's choices, which cannot be wholly predicted.

Contrast. Tracy and Levinsohn offer the following example of -*ri* on an adjective to show contrast (their example 2). Similar examples occur in my corpus but are rare.

(425) *in?gui -ri péri -ri tikeki nʌža*
one TOP dog TOP behind walk
Certain dogs walk behind;

(426) *ei aw -e? -ri in?gui -ri peri umʌn sanusi*
thus AUX then TOP one TOP dog more ahead

zei-n nʌ-ngua a?zina
go-IMPF 1O-FUT think
Other dogs want to go further ahead.

Thematic participant. -*ri* on nouns sets a phrase apart within the clause, often in clause-initial position, as topic, theme, or point of departure for what follows. Tracy and Levinsohn describe this function as marking the THEMATIC PARTICIPANT of the paragraph. Their analysis leans heavily on the notion of the grammatical paragraph, a concept that is problematic in practical terms, even if one subscribes to the notion that the paragraph is a grammatical unit. That is, the presence of -*ri* may help identify a stretch of talk that has coherence around the topic so marked, but it is more doubtful that one could identify the paragraphs and then use that information to help determine the placement of -*ri*.

Contrastive topic. A close examination of the contexts in which *-ri* marks noun phrases reveals a number of conditions on its use:

a. *-ri* marks NPs referring to entities which are given information or, more specifically, to ones which are either evoked (previously mentioned in the linguistic context or present in the situational context) or inferrable (whose existence can be inferred on the basis of other entities established in the discourse; cf. Prince 1980).

b. *-ri* is contrastive in that it marks one out of a set of possible referents.

c. Assuming NP-*ri* to be a marked topic, the corresponding comment must also in some sense be contrastive or particularly noteworthy.

The first condition refers to the status of the entity concerned in the discourse. A noun phrase marked by *-ri* concerns something already known and presumably of more than passing interest in the discourse. In terms of Hopper and Thompson 1984, it must be discourse manipulable, i.e., it must play a role in the discourse and be salient or prominent. The implication is that first references to participants are not candidates for marking by *-ri*. Cases which appear to involve *-ri* in first references usually turn out to involve (a) references which only APPEAR to be first references because the text has been removed from the interactional context in which it was elicited, or (b) references to inferrable entities. An example of the latter is dogs in hunting stories. One element of the hunting script for speakers of Ika would be that hunting dogs are used to track the quarry, thus invoking the hunting script in a narrative would make the presence of dogs a straightforward inference, such that the first overt reference to dogs can nonetheless treat them as given information.

The use of *-ri* usually involves contrast, and the entity marked is usually one of several possible referents. What is predicated about the entity highlighted by *-ri* must also be particularly noteworthy and is often in contrast with what is known about the other possible referents. Thus, *-ri* is usually used to shift focus from one participant or prop to another and also serves to highlight what is predicated about that entity.

The following passage illustrates this shifting of focus between participants on stage in a narrative, along with their contrasting actions. *José-ri* is advised not to join in on a hunt, and he goes one way while *Pedru* and *Rafa-ri* head off in the other direction.

(427) *Jose -ri   Pédru -sin   ʌn-zuei-ʔ nar   -i   -ri,   Ariguaní*
     Jose TOP Pedro with REF-go-NEG AUX while TOP Ariguaní

   a-žuna   ʌžá-rigʌn   zʌn? monu   tšai-n   zoža-na
   ʔ-goˆdown that-LOC   just   monkey shoot-IMPF go-DIST
   José didn't go with Pedro but went down to Ariguaní to hunt monkeys.

(428) *ei   u-ž   -eʔ   -ri   iwa   Pédru -ri   Rafa a -sin -di*
     thus AUX-MED then TOP now Pedro TOP Rafa 3 with TOP

   gunn-i win-deʔs -i   ri-zoža kinki   u-na   ni
   hand   3pS-agree while 3pS-go   really AUX-DIST CERT

   Potreru ra   Tšákʌra ažá-rigʌn
   Potrero la   Chacra   that-LOC
   And so Pedro and Rafa decided to go to Potrero la Chacra.

-ri is probably best seen as establishing a sentence topic rather than a discourse topic because of the other rapid shifts of attention from one participant to another in a short stretch of text. As will be argued below, zero anaphora is the best indicator of discourse topicality (§9.5) while *-ri* functions on a more local level to help signal topic-comment structuring within a clause. These topic-comment structures, however, may in turn serve to highlight focal observations about or actions of the participant around which a stretch of text revolves, thus helping to explain Tracy and Levinsohn's observation that *-ri* marks the thematic participant for a paragraph.

This analysis of *-ri* as marking CONTRASTIVE TOPIC is related to Tracy and Levinsohn's observation that *-ri* on adjectives signals contrast. The connection between *-ri* on noun phrase (or adjective) and *-ri* marking the end of a dependent clause may not be as obvious but is similar to what Haiman describes for Hua (a Papuan language), in which the same suffix is used both clause-finally to indicate conditional as well as to mark contrastive topics. Haiman (1978:583) analyzes the function common to both uses as constituting "the Framework which has been selected for the following discourse." Clause-final *-ri* could be described similarly; in marking progression in narrative, it helps mark events upon which the subsequent discourse builds.

9.8. Participant reference. Participant reference can be taken as the set of principles that govern or influence the choice of means by which entities are referred to in discourse. The term REFERRED TO must be interpreted broadly enough to include zero anaphora—cases in which an entity is not overtly mentioned in a clause but is part of the case frame of the verb. In Ika, there are essentially three choices for participant reference: (a) an unmarked noun phrase, (b) a noun phrase marked by -*ri* (topic), and (c) zero anaphora. After first summarizing Tracy and Levinsohn's observations concerning participant reference in expository discourse, I present some quantitative data concerning the use of these three means of reference. I conclude that unmarked noun phrases are used for participants which are nontopical and which usually have a short-term presence in the discourse; that zero anaphora is the usual means for referring to topical and given participants; and that -*ri* marks noun phrases that refer to topical participants in cases where an overt noun phrase is needed to make reference clear.

Tracy and Levinsohn summarize the patterns of participant reference as follows. Participants are divided into two basic sets—thematic and non-thematic within a given stretch of text. Thematic participants can only be ones that occupy a significant discourse role (usually the central character or some character related to the central character). The thematic participant is indicated by -*ri* attached to the end of the noun phrase which refers to the participant, in the opening sentence of each new paragraph (1977:8). Within the body of the paragraph, there is no overt reference to the thematic participant (zero anaphora). In the final sentence of a paragraph, all three means of referring to participants may be used with the thematic participant—overt reference with or without -*ri*, or zero anaphora. Nonthematic participants are handled by means of overt noun phrases unmarked by -*ri*: "the presence of a nonthematic participant in a paragraph is indicated by his being overtly mentioned, but the reference carries no -*ri* marker" (1977:8).

Topic continuity. Givón has suggested that there are three types of main topics in thematic paragraphs ("a string of clauses whose main/primary topic remains the same" 1983:9) and relates these types to the degree to which the entity involved is relatively continuous or discontinuous with the preceding and following discourse context. The three types of main topics are:

(a) Chain initial topic:
(i) Characteristically a newly-introduced or newly-returned topic; thus
(ii) Characteristically a discontinuous topic in terms of the preceding discourse context; but

(iii) Potentially—if an important topic—a rather persistent topic in terms of the succeeding discourse context.

(b) Chain medial topic:
 (i) Characteristically a continuing/continuous topic in terms of the preceding discourse context; and also
 (ii) Characteristically persistent—but not maximally so—in terms of the succeeding discourse context, even when an important topic.

(c) Chain final topic:
 (i) Characteristically a continuing/continuous topic in terms of the preceding discourse context; but
 (ii) Characteristically a nonpersistent topic in terms of the succeeding discourse context, even if an important topic (1983:9).

Two tests which Givón suggests for measuring the continuity of topics in discourse involve referential distance back to the last reference to the topic, and the topic's persistence in the following discourse context. Givón describes referential distance as follows

> This measurement assesses the gap between the previous occurrence in the discourse of a referent/topic and its current occurrence in a clause, where it is marked by a particular grammatical coding device. The gap is thus expressed in terms of number of clauses to the left (1983:13).

Topics which are more discontinuous with respect to the preceding discourse context have a higher referential distance. The measure that Givón suggests for persistence in the subsequent discourse involves:

> the number of clauses to the right—i.e. in subsequent discourse from the measured clause—in which the topic/participant continues an uninterrupted presence as a semantic argument of the clause, an argument of whatever role and marked by whatever grammatical means (1983:15).

These measures help determine the relative (dis)continuity of available grammatical devices for coding topics and thus enable one to make conclusions regarding the function of the available devices in marking the different types of topics listed above.

Topic continuity in Ika discourse. In order to measure topic continuity in Ika discourse, I have examined noun phrases, noun phrases plus *-ri*, and zero anaphora in an eleven-clause window of text—the preceding and succeeding five clauses around a given clause. I used a narrative and an expositorytext, totaling 113 clauses and 169 references to participants. For each participant identifiable as part of the case frame of a verb, I noted the grammatical means of referring to that participant and the participant's presence in the preceding and following five clauses. In the tables below, the grammatical means are given as NP (unmarked noun phrase), *-ri* (noun phrase plus *-ri* (topic)), and ∅ (zero anaphora). (429) lists the average number of clauses back to the last occurrence of the participant for the three coding devices. Note that an unmarked noun phrase shows the most discontinuity with the previous context (highest average distance back to last occurrence), that zero anaphora shows the most continuity with the previous context (lowest average distance back to last occurrence), and that noun phrases marked by *-ri* stand in between the two.

(429) Average distance back to last occurrence
 NP 4.33 clauses
 -ri 2.61 clauses
 ∅ 1.43 clauses

Thus, zero anaphora occurs with topics that have usually been mentioned in the immediately prior discourse context, relative to topics referred to by noun phrases. In addition, *-ri* occurs on noun phrases in situations involving greater continuity with the previous context, relative to unmarked noun phrases. This provides additional confirmation that *-ri* only occurs with given information (§9.7).

The average number of clauses in which a participant has an uninterrupted presence in subsequent discourse, according to the grammatical encoding device, is listed in (430). Zero anaphora shows the greatest continuity in the following context, unmarked noun phrases show the least persistence, and, again, noun phrases marked by *-ri* show an intermediate amount of persistence.

(430) Persistence of topics in subsequent discourse.
 NP .98 clauses
 -ri 1.41 clauses
 ∅ 2.18 clauses

These two sets of figures give support to Tracy and Levinsohn's observations on participant reference. The minor role of participants referenced by unmarked noun phrases is seen in the relatively long distance back to a last reference and the short amount of uninterrupted presence in the following discourse.[41] The evidence concerning -*ri* is not conclusive with regard to the concept of marking the thematic participant of a paragraph, but the figures do show that noun phrases marked by -*ri* have a greater degree of continuity with respect to the following discourse than unmarked noun phrases. The data also show that zero anaphora codes established topics, as seen in the high degree of continuity in both preceding and following discourse.

In relation to Givón's types of main topics, above, zero anaphora is the preferred encoding device for chain-medial topics, having relatively high continuity with both prior and following contexts. -*ri* would seem to be the device for encoding chain-initial topics, showing greater discontinuity with the prior contexts than zero anaphora but more persistence than unmarked noun phrases. Zero anaphora seems a better indicator of discourse topicality than -*ri*, suggesting that -*ri* is more of a sentence topic marker. Since -*ri* marks entities which are of more than passing interest in the discourse, however, the entities it marks have greater persistence in subsequent text than do unmarked noun phrases. Unmarked noun phrases would seem to be the means for encoding minor topics rather than major ones. On the whole, they show relatively little continuity in text, which is an indication of their minor pragmatic status. This study does not shed light on the matter of chain-final topics, but it appears that this is one area in which word order interacts with topic continuity. I commented above that postverbal subjects often involve participants that are moving off a scene (§9.6.). In particular, chain-final topics appear to be ones that are both postposed and marked by -*ri*.

9.9. Optional auxiliary verbs and pragmatic structuring. In the discussion above (§5.1) of optional auxiliary verbs in the verb phrase, I suggested that optional auxiliaries serve a pragmatic function of highlighting the lexical verb. This analysis rests in part on a conception of the pragmatic structuring of Ika clauses. In §9.8, I used the term TOPIC in a very general sense—any entity which plays a role in a clause. One may also speak of the topic of a clause as a particular item around which the clause

---

[41]The higher figure for referential distance with unmarked noun phrases is partly due to the fact that first introductions of participants yield the highest amount of distance (with 6 clauses as the maximum number in my study) and unmarked noun phrases are the basic choice for the first mention of a participant.

revolves, the item that the clause is 'about'. Topics in this latter sense are usually considered to be given information and definite. I stated above that zero anaphora is the usual means for referring to such topics, with -*ri* specifically marking noun phrases as topical for those cases in which an overt noun phrase is needed. In this sense, a starting point for considering the pragmatic structure of Ika clauses is to recognize topic versus comment, and marked topics (-*ri*) versus unmarked topics (zero anaphora). My conclusion concerning optional auxiliary verbs is that they produce a marked structure in the comment portion of a clause, highlighting the lexical verb itself.

Dooley (1982) investigates the tendency to use constituent structure in Guaraní to show pragmatic structure and suggests that all languages will similarly have some indication of pragmatic structure. He holds that in pragmatic terms, Guaraní sentences may be divided up into various constituents such as connectives, settings, topic, and a pragmatic nucleus (the only obligatory part of the utterance). Dooley's discussion of pragmatically marked structures in Guaraní shows parallels to the Ika use of optional auxiliary verbs:

> Marked pragmatic structuring can be produced in Guaraní in several ways. By far the most common means is a marked expression: an expression becomes marked when (a final segment of) the pragmatic nucleus is given a binary constituent structure which highlights that expression. This binary constituent structure is prominently indicated by marked word-order, intonation, or other special features, with the marked expression as one constituent. I will call the other, non-highlighted constituent the remainder constituent. The marked expression always precedes the remainder constituent; and this may be the general rule for languages in which marked expressions occur (1982:312).

My analysis of optional auxiliary verbs in Ika is that they serve to produce pragmatically marked expressions having a binary constituent structure, with the lexical verb as the marked expression and the optional auxiliary verb and the rest of the verb phrase as the nonhighlighted, remainder constituent.

Dooley notes that for Guaraní the usual pragmatic nucleus is an unmarked topic plus core, the core being "roughly described as the most informative pragmatic component" (1982:310). I suggest that a similar situation holds with Ika clauses. A noun phrase marked by -*ri* serves as a marked topic and participants referenced by zero anaphora serve as unmarked topics, with the rest of the clause serving as the core. Verb phrases with optional auxiliaries represent a marked core, highlighting the verb as the most informative part of the clause, leaving auxiliary verb(s) with the rest of the information in the clause as the 'remainder constituent'. Much remains to be done in this area, but an example will help indicate the direction in which this analysis is pointing.

Illustration (431) contains three clauses in two sentences. The first clause has a ∅ subject as unmarked topic and otherwise only a verb phrase. The verb phrase contains an optional auxiliary, highlighting the verb as the informationally most important element in the clause. The second and third clauses, in the second sentence, each contain a marked topic noun phrase followed by an unmarked core. Note that in each of these clauses, it is the locative word and not the verb that is informationally most important, and that the verb phrase does not contain an auxiliary. Marked noun phrases focus on the contrast in participants involved, and the rest of each clause gives details concerning the participant in focus. The brackets indicate my conception of the pragmatic constituency of each clause.

(431) [TOPIC]   [MARKED-CORE   REMAINDER]
      [∅]   *[zoža   u-na]*
      (they)   go   AUX-DIST
      They went.

   [MARKED TOPIC]   [CORE]
   [a -ri]   *[meina   keiwɨ   zori   -eʔ   -ri]*
   he   TOP   stream right^away   go   then   TOP
   He went along a stream,

   [MARKED TOPIC]   [CORE]
   [mouga -ri]   *[awaʔrei zoža-na]*
   two   TOP   below   go-DIST
   and the other two went along below.

Optional auxiliaries are found most frequently in clauses containing only a verb phrase—clear cases of the verb being the informationally most important part of the proposition. This marked structure is found less often with verb phrases which already have an obligatory auxiliary verb, possibly because such a phrase already has the lexical verb separated toward the left and the rest of the grammatical material to the right on an obligatory auxiliary verb. There would be less need in such cases to create a marked structure in order to highlight the lexical verb. Firmer conclusions concerning optional auxiliary verbs and pragmatic structuring will have to await a separate study.

10
Conclusion

No language has ever been completely described, and relatively few have been described in any detail when one considers the total number of languages in the world. This grammar of Ika is intended not to give the final word on the language but to offer a first, broad treatment of grammatical phenomena for Ika. All conclusions in preceding sections should be treated as suggestive and in need of further investigation, even though I have attempted to be as accurate and complete as possible within the constraints of my data base and an imperfect grasp of the language. I hope that further research will result in the correction of errors and shed further light on the many fascinating phenomena that I have seen without yet being able to fully understand. Several major areas definitely warrant further investigation. The morphophonemic system is one of these areas, and an adequate analysis of Ika morphophonemics will necessitate compiling data on the alternative forms of a large number of roots and the majority of the affixes to enable the formulation of generalizations concerning patterns of interaction between morphemes in combination.

There are a number of details concerning the clause level that need additional work. Chief among these matters, in my mind, are the pragmatic factors concerning zero anaphora, the ubiquitous enclitic -*ri*, word order, and optional auxiliary verbs. Clearly, much of the work in this area will have to be discourse-based and would benefit from observation of language in use by the Bíntukwa in everyday interaction.

Complex sentence structures form another area in which much more work is needed. My intention has been to present at least the basics of Ika syntax with a view to creating an interest among syntacticians in the syntax of relatively little-known languages. Specialized techniques will be necessary to secure the evidence needed from otherwise infrequently occurring structures such as verbal complements and relative clauses.

I have given no systematic attention in this study to the whole question of discourse genre and ways of speaking. There is firm evidence that the type of discourse and the social setting for talk have a effect on the grammatical structures that will be found in the data (for example, cf. Schieffelin 1979). Thus, perhaps the greatest need, in order to make further progress in understanding Ika grammar, is to supplement the data base so as to ensure a corpus that is representative of the way that Ika is used in a wide range of social circumstances, including, especially, observations of language in use in situations where language itself is not in focus (cf. Labov 1975 on the limitations of the normal procedures used in descriptive fieldwork).

The Ika language deserves the additional research that I have outlined here as well as in other areas. I hope that this study will serve as a foundation for such research and will stimulate corrections as well as extensions into new areas of the grammar.

Bibliography

Allen, Barbara J., Donna B. Gardiner, and Donald G. Frantz. 1984. Noun incorporation in Southern Tiwa. International Journal of American Linguistics 50:292–311.

Blake, Barry J. 1977. Case marking in Australian languages. (Australian Institute of Aboriginal Studies, Linguistic Series No. 23). Canberra: Australian Institute of Aboriginal Studies.

Comrie, Bernard. 1981a. Language universals and linguistic typology. Chicago: University of Chicago Press.

———. 1981b. Tense. Cambridge: Cambridge University Press.

———, and Edward L. Keenan. 1979. Noun phrase accessibility revisited. Language 55:649–64.

Constenla Umaña, Adolfo. 1981. Comparative Chibchan phonology. Ph.D. thesis, University of Pennsylvania.

———. 1982. Sobre la construcción ergativa en la lengua guatusa. Revista de Filología y Lingüística de la Universidad de Costa Rica 8:97–101.

DeLancey, Scott. 1981. An interpretation of split ergativity and related patterns. Language 57:626–57.

Dixon, R. M. W. (ed.). 1976. Grammatical categories in Australian languages. Australian Institute of Aboriginal Studies, Linguistic Series No. 22. Canberra: Australian Institute of Aboriginal Studies.

———. 1979. Ergativity. Language 55:59–138.

———. 1982. Where have all the adjectives gone. Berlin: Mouton.

Dooley, Robert A. 1982. Options in the pragmatic structuring of Guarani sentences. Language 58:307–31.

Fillmore, Charles J. 1975. Santa Cruz lectures on deixis, 1971. Bloomington: Indiana University Press.

Givón, Talmy (ed.). 1983. Topic continuity in discourse: quantitative cross-language studies. Amsterdam: John Benjamins.

———. 1984. Syntax I, a functional-typological introduction. Amsterdam: John Benjamins.

Greenberg, Joseph H. 1966. Some universals of grammar with particular reference to the order of meaningful elements. In Greenberg (ed.), Universals of language, 73–133. Cambridge, Mass.: MIT Press.

Grimes, Joesph E. 1972. Outlines and overlays. Language 48:513–24.

Haiman, John. 1978. Conditionals are topics. Language 54:564–89.

Hopper, Paul J., and Sandra A. Thompson. 1980. Transitivity in syntax and discourse. Language 56:251–299.

——— and ———. 1984. The discourse basis for lexical categories in universal grammar. Language 60:703–52.

Hudson, Grover. 1980. Automatic alternations in non-transformational phonology. Language 56:94–125.

Issacs, Jorge. 1884. Estudio sobre las tribus indígenas del estado del Magdalena antes provincia de Santa Marta. Anales de la Instrucción Pública de los Estados Unidos de Colombia 8(45):177–352.

Jijón y Caamaño, Jacinto. 1943. Las lenguas del sur de Centro América y el norte y centro del oeste de Sud-América. El Ecuador Interandino y Occidental 3 Quito: Editorial Ecuatoriana.

Key, Mary Ritchie. 1979. The grouping of American Indian languages. (Ars Linguistica 2). Tübingen: Gunter Narr Verlag.

Labov, William. 1975. What is a linguistic fact? Lisse: Peter de Ridder Press.

Landaburu, Jon. 1985. La construcción de la referencia del sujeto en Ika (Arhuaco de la Sierra Nevada de Santa Marta). Paper presented at the XLV Congress of Americanists, Bogotá, 1985.

Lehmann, Winfred P. 1972. Converging theories in linguistics. Language 48:266–75.

———. 1978. The great underlying ground-plans. In Lehmann (ed.), Syntactic typology: studies in the phenomenology of language, 3–56. Austin: University of Texas Press.

Longacre, Robert E. 1972. Hierarchy and universality of discourse constituents in New Guinea languages: discussion. Washington, D.C.: Georgetown University Press.

Loukotka, Cestmir. 1935. Clasificación de las lenguas sudaméricas. Prague.

———. 1938. Intrusión de las idiomas Centro-Américas en América del Sur. Anales de la Universidad de Nariño 2:243–64.

———. 1968. Classification of South American Indian languages. Los Angeles: UCLA Latin American Center.

Mason, John. 1950. The Languages of South American Indians. In J. Steward (ed.), Handbook of South American Indians 6:157–317.

McQuown, Norman A. 1955. The indigenous languages of Latin America. American Anthropologist 57:501–70.

Prince, Ellen F. 1980. Towards a taxonomy of given—new information. In Peter Cole (ed.), Radical pragmatics, 223–56. New York: Academic Press.

Reichenbach, Hans. 1947. Elements of symbolic logic. New York: New York Free Press.

Rivet, Paul, and Cestmir Loukotka. 1952. Langues de l© Amerique du Sud et des Antilles. In A. Meillet and M. Cohen (eds.), Les langues du monde, 110–600. Paris: Centre National de la Recherche Scientifique.

Schieffelin, Bambi. 1979. How Kaluli children learn what to say, what to do, and how to feel: An ethnographic study of the development of communicative competence. Ph.D. thesis, Columbia University.

Shafer, Robert. 1962. Aruakan (not Arawakan). Anthropological Linguistics 4:4:31–40.

Silverstein, Michael. 1976. Hierarchy of features and ergativity. In Dixon (ed.), 112–71.

Stout, Mickey, and Ruth Thomson. 1971. Kayapó narrative. International Journal of American Linguistics 37:250–56.

Tovar, Antonio. 1961. Catálogo de las lenguas de América del Sur. Buenos Aires: Editorial Sudamérica.

Tracy, Hubert P., and Stephen H. Levinsohn. 1977. Participant reference in Ica expository discourse. In R. E. Longacre and F. Woods (eds.), Discourse grammar: studies in indigenous languages of Colombia, Panama, and Ecuador, 3-24. Publications in linguistics 52. Dallas: Summer Institute of Linguistics and the University of Texas at Arlington.

——, and Martha Tracy. 1973. Fonemas del ica. Sistemas fonológicos de idiomas colombianos 2: 57-70. Lomalinda, Meta, Colombia: Instituto Lingüístico de Verano.

Wheeler, Alva. 1972. Proto Chibchan. In Esther Matteson, et al. (eds.), Comparative studies in Amerindian languages. 93-108. The Hague: Mouton.

Vinalesa, Padre José de. 1952. Indios Arhuacos de la Sierra Nevada de Santa Marta. Bogotá: Editorial Iqueima.

www.ingramcontent.com/pod-product-compliance
Lightning Source LLC
Chambersburg PA
CBHW051102230426
43667CB00013B/2409